ACADEMIC LIBRARY BUILDINGS

Academic Library Buildings

A GUIDE TO ARCHITECTURAL ISSUES AND SOLUTIONS

Ralph E. Ellsworth

Director of Libraries and Professor of Bibliography Emeritus
The University of Colorado

THE COLORADO ASSOCIATED UNIVERSITY PRESS
BOULDER, COLORADO 1973

Contents

Foreword

THE quarter of a century since the end of World War II has been unique in the history of academic library construction. Concrete, steel, and dreams converged on campuses across North America creating an unprecedented quantity of new library facilities.

Indeed, the past five years alone could qualify as the Golden Age of library-building. Assisted by federal subsidies and loans, four-year colleges and universities in the United States built a record 450 libraries at a cost of almost a billion dollars. We are not likely to see soon again, if ever, such remarkable expansion in so brief a period. Still, there are buildings to be built and building decisions to be made.

The estimates are that construction will stabilize at a level of some 50 new buildings a year for some time to come, with activity concentrated in undergraduate library facilities, two-year colleges, remodelings, and additions.

The recently built libraries provide a rich resource of architectural solutions to the problems peculiar to academic library buildings. They express the work of talented architects, planners, consultants, and librarians who devoted themselves to the creation of structures that would grace their campuses spiritually as well as physically, and would efficiently serve the purposes of learning. They incorporate a broad variety of physical styles, theories of library management, organizations of library materials and services, and types of furniture and equipment.

Because these buildings serve as a history of the past and a guide to the future, it seemed to us appropriate that the wealth of experience they embody should be assembled in a comprehensive report.

This book is the product of such an effort. It is an annotated photographic record (some 1500 photos) of 130 academic libraries. It is not intended to be a select sampling of the very best or the most elegant. (Where, in any case, would one find two critics who might agree?) It is, rather, a working manual, a journeyman's guide to the physical decisions made by planners in the resolution of issues peculiar to libraries. The emphasis is on specific functional elements so that readers concerned with a particular problem — reference, perhaps, or microforms, or any other functional category — can learn how the matter was resolved in a variety of libraries ranging across the United States, Canada, Great Britain, and Western Europe. Geographic coverage seemed important, both to capture regional flavor (where it still exists), and because readers may wish to see first-hand, in their own localities, some of the examples.

Educational Facilities Laboratories and the Council on Library Resources are indebted to Dr. Ralph E. Ellsworth, Director of Libraries at the University of Colorado, who worked harder than one should in a sabbatical year, visiting hundreds of libraries, photographing the good things he saw, and writing this book. Responsibility for the selection of materials, the photographs, and for the text, rests solely with him and not with the staffs of EFL or the Council.

Hopefully, this chronicle will help planners develop even better libraries and will direct attention to those matters that need further analysis and research. We hope, moreover, that it will be helpful to the designers and manufacturers of furniture and equipment who are engaged in a search for better ways to meet the developing needs of the electronic age and of micro-publishing.

And finally, to paraphrase Descartes — it is not enough to have a good book; the main thing is to use it well.

Educational Facilities Laboratories
and
The Council on Library Resources

April 1972

Preface

THIS book attempts to present representative examples of successful architectural solutions to the important problems librarians and architects face in planning new college and university library buildings or in remodeling and enlarging existing structures. It does not attempt to make case study evaluations, as was done by Ellsworth Mason for Brown and Yale.[1] Nor does it present examples of unsuccessful solutions except to show how to avoid mistakes, and in these cases the libraries will not be identified.

I set out to visit and photograph all the new buildings, mostly less than five years old, in the United States, Canada, England, Scotland, France, Germany, and Sweden, that had been reported by my colleagues to be good buildings, or at least to have some good features. However, as the year wore on so did I; and since I had left the eastern part of the United States until last, I had to be more selective among the new libraries in that part of the country than I was in the west. I should have included more of the state colleges in New York and Pennsylvania. Several specific omissions weigh heavily on my conscience: Wabash, Antioch, Berea, Michigan State University at Lansing, Southern Illinois University, the science library at Hanover University in Germany, and the Technical University in Helsinki, Finland. Nevertheless, the list included is extensive enough to serve the purpose of presenting good examples for all parts of the country.

1. Mason, Ellsworth, "Beinecke Siamese Twins . . . ," *College and Research Libraries*, 26:199–212, May 1965, and "The Rock . . . ," *Library Journal*, 93:4487–92, December 1, 1968.

Several buildings under construction were not completed in time to make our deadline: New York University and the University of Massachusetts were the two largest that could not be included. The new Southern Methodist University Law Library will, in action, be the outstanding law library in the United States.

The procedure used in choosing the buildings to be included was as follows. I first wrote to some one hundred academic librarians, architects, and planners asking them to list the new buildings they considered successful from a functional point of view. Next I checked the last five years of *Library Literature*. Finally, using my own rather extensive files, I coordinated all of this information and divided the country into geographic areas that could be covered in two-week trips — that being as long as I could travel at one time. I analyzed and photographed the buildings I visited. In between trips I had four-by-six-inch prints made of the films. Each was identified, labeled, and classified into a master index by type of planning problem.

The first part of each chapter will state as briefly as possible the architectural and planning issues. Following the text the annotated photographs will attempt to show the various ways architects have met these issues. The pictures are arranged by state and country.

A word about the photography. These are librarians' working pictures intended to show what the subject looks like. They are not the work of a professional photographer. Even though the presence of people in a photograph usually makes it more interesting, I found that one could capture the scene better without people, except when they were needed to show scale. Yet the temptation to include a pretty face, figure, or an action scene was not always resisted. Mrs. Ellsworth helped me with the composition of many of the pictures. Photographs have their limitations, as do words and blueprints, therefore I have included floor plans. I have included only enough text to state the architectural issues involved and to explain matters that are not clear from the photographs. Three cameras were used: a Mamiya-Sekor 1000 with a wide angle lens, a Yashika 72 half frame, and a Minolta 500 for a few color photographs. I hope the reader will not be too critical of exterior shots where the walls of tall buildings curve, or of interiors where the chairs were not neatly arranged. I made my pictures as I saw the scene, not always as the camera saw it; we did not always agree. Credit is given for pictures taken by photographers. Some were taken by me on earlier trips.

Early in the selection process I discovered that there was little agreement among my colleagues about the merits and demerits of specific buildings; and, knowing how much librarians disagree among themselves about philosophies of library services, I was not too surprised. I assume full responsibility for the choices made.

My own biases, insofar as I know them, are as follows. I have looked for buildings that house library activities well and that meet the criteria for judging a building already stated by Keyes Metcalf and myself and others in our books. I tend to rate highly the lean and hungry buildings and to discount those that are fat with useless architectural flourishes. This is not a matter of aesthetic Puritanism but rather a tentative conviction that the latter tend to be fashions that have a short life. I judge the beauty of a building the same way I do the beauty of a woman — she must be structurally sound, must move well, and should have interesting texture. The rest is secondary. Mere prettiness can be achieved by the use of tricks and gadgets.

But I see no reason why a college or university, if it knows what it is doing and can afford it, cannot employ an architect who lays on all the architectural niceties he can, provided the building still meets the essential criteria for functioning.

There are other points of view on the aesthetics of library architecture, naturally. Ralph D. Thomson, Director of Libraries, University of Utah, has stated one such point of view very well:

> On the other hand, I contend that beauty in a building, even if it seems impractical, has a function that cannot be overlooked. Also, the size of a building has something to do with the need for such things as atriums and so-called monumental stairways. There must be plenty of stairway and elevator facilities to move large numbers of people without crowding. While providing this necessary space, it might as well be made beautiful. An atrium in a small building is not the same thing from a functional consideration as when the building is large and there needs to be some area where there can be a point when one part of the building can be related to the balance of the space in the building. This is especially true where there are large areas on each floor and where there are few outside windows.

Some of my friends are surer than I am about their ability to identify beauty in architecture and furniture. And some of them even claim that Victorian furniture is nice to have around even though they admit it is uncomfortable to sit on. To me a library is a workshop, a studio, a laboratory, not an art museum.

I have tried to remember that a library building is not a library but merely a place where libraries are housed.

I have tried also to remember that we are in the very early stages of a communication revolution, the implications of which for library planning could be very extensive and could also leach out into minor readjustments.

The processes of choosing the pictures to use from the file of thousands makes me uneasy about my sins of omission. For each example selected there were a dozen or more equally good. I regret they could not all have been included, and I hope I have not disappointed too many librarians and architects, who, justifiably, may feel that their buildings are just as good as those selected for inclusion.

During the course of the I.F.L.A. Colloquium on the Construction of University Library Buildings held in Lausanne, Switzerland, in June, 1971, it became clear to me that my coverage of the new German University library buildings was inadequate. I have seen the plans for those German buildings not included in this study, and while they are interesting from an architectural point of view they are organized on a philosophy of service no longer practiced in the United States. For that reason I have not felt it worthwhile to postpone the publication of this study in order to include those buildings.

Finally, I wish to express my appreciation to the University of Colorado for allowing me to spend the year traveling, and to the Educational Facilities Laboratories, Inc., for the grant which made this study possible.

Ralph E. Ellsworth

How to Use this Book

THIS is intended to be a source book of information on how the new library buildings are planned, arranged, and equipped. Each photograph was selected to illustrate one point, but, obviously, there is usually more than one thing to see in each photograph. It did not seem necessary for me to point out these things, except in a few cases.

Photographs of furniture, equipment, bookstacks, etc. can be found in manufacturers' catalogs. This book shows how the equipment, etc. is used in real library working environments.

The reason for arranging the photographs by state and country under each topic is to provide a handy guide to good examples in each part of the country so that architects, librarians and committees may find out which libraries they should visit, in their own area if possible. This causes some duplication in the displays. I could have developed a system of cross references tied to a single arrangement of the pictures, but this would have sent the reader scurrying back and forth through the book. I avoided that.

The chapters on reader stations and book handling could have been merged, but were kept separate even though the differences between the two sometimes became a matter of emphasis rather than uniqueness. This was done to save the time of the reader, and also, I suppose, to justify a larger display of examples.

The book does not attempt, except for pointing out blatant errors, to measure the success or degree of acceptability of the new buildings. It is time now that such evaluations be undertaken, because we now have enough examples of various kinds of practices to justify generalizations. However, for the reasons stated in the Conclusions About Planning, this kind of analysis should be approached with great caution and wisdom.

For each photograph used in the book there are probably ten more in my files — arranged in envelopes by name of institution. This file is freely available. The microfilm negatives are also available. Enlarged prints can be made by the University of Colorado Photograph Laboratory upon demand.

A method of keeping the files up to date is being studied.

Entrance, Washington University

I

Library System Profiles

SINCE the American university is a combination of the American liberal arts college (a unique institution) and the German type of graduate plus professional school mixed in with some Hochschule curricula, it is not surprising that the American library system carries a mixed heritage.

Most small and medium-sized liberal arts colleges have a central library building with no formally administered or recognized departmental libraries. However, departmental reading rooms with a few current journals are not uncommon in the science buildings. In the larger colleges, the departmental reading rooms are usually larger and may even be officially recognized as departmental libraries. This is especially true in those liberal arts colleges that offer graduate work, such as Oberlin or Dartmouth.

In the older, larger universities, the German system of a central library plus many departmental libraries of all kinds and sizes has been omnipresent, resulting from the fact that most university faculties did their graduate work in German universities around the turn of the century. Most are administered through the central library but a few follow the older German pattern of independent faculty libraries. The central library, since it contains the liberal arts college library, is usually stronger and larger in terms of its human population than is the older German university central library, which sometimes serves as the state library also. In the newer American universities and in some of the older ones fortunate enough to have grown beyond the limits of their older campuses, and thus to have had the chance to locate faculty departments

on a basis of some intellectual logic, all the libraries — except
law, which is always separate, and medicine, which is frequently
located in another city — are sometimes located in the central
library building. A single science library instead of a series of departmental libraries is not uncommon. And professional school libraries
for music and art and architecture are sometimes present. The
college, or undergraduate, library, designed to handle the large
numbers of undergraduates, has been in vogue since World War
II, although there is little agreement among librarians as to the
real purpose of these libraries. Emory University, for example,
places all materials for assigned readings in their old library building
and everything that is unassigned, or on an independent study
basis, in the new general library. Most undergraduate libraries
are located very close to the main building, if they are not a part
of it physically, because there is usually a 25 percent interchange
of use between the two kinds.

Dormitory or house libraries exist in only a few of the older
and more wealthy private universities such as Harvard, Yale, and
Rice. But the hue and cry against impersonality in the large state
university has caused renewed interest in the residential college
idea, exemplified by the University of California in Santa Cruz.
Universities like Northern Illinois University which have constructed residential centers housing up to 5,000 residents at some distance from the central campus can be expected to supply some
kind of library service to residents of those dormitories.

In England and Scotland the new Robbins, or provincial universities, have been greatly influenced by the new American centralized plan with strong emphasis on the central library and with
de-emphasis on the departmental libraries. These can be found
in such places as Lancaster, Warwick, Kent, Essex, Sussex, East
Anglia, York, etc. Edinburgh and Glasgow, both old and prestigious
universities, have large new central library buildings; and even
though departmental libraries still exist on those campuses, there
is a high degree of coordination among them.

In France on the newer campuses, several patterns exist. Caen
and Lyon, for example, both have large single central library buildings. In Aix-en-Province there are two main libraries — one for
the social sciences and one for the humanities. In the University
of Marseille there are two — Social Science and Science. The
same pattern exists at the University of Nice.

In Germany, most of the universities now have large new central libraries, but in most of these universities the science faculty libraries are not included in the central buildings. The same is true in Scandinavia.

In Canada, in the newer universities, central libraries of an inclusive kind exist, such as Guelph University, the University of Waterloo, Simon Frasier University, etc. And in the older universities the systems are decentralized.

Other countries have not been included in this report.

In the United States, at least, the profile of the library system in our universities is highly mobile and is quickly influenced by such forces as the highly developed inter-disciplinary relationships among the sciences and more recently within the behavioral sciences. These intellectual forces seem to be forcing the development of a larger grouping of small departmental libraries in a single building. One finds widespread belief that soon the computer will bring to the desk of each scientist the information he wants, thus making the location of the books or the carriers of this information relatively unimportant — except for the current issues of the journals a scientist must examine for close "current awareness."

And, of course, the new ultramicrofiche may change the patterns of library service, if publishers expand the scope of their projects. (See "Libraries in Miniature: A New Era Begins" by John Tebbel in *The Saturday Review*, January 9, 1971, pp. 41–42.) Lack of attention to user needs on the part of promoters, publishers, and machine designers perhaps explains why readers have not willingly accepted microforms as a substitute for the printed page. Prototypes by the Library Materials and Manufacturing Co. and in the Barker Library at Massachusetts Institute of Technology show considerable promise.

Old and New, Guelph University

II

Trends and Dilemmas

PRIOR to World War II all academic libraries were planned on a fixed-function basis. After World War II the American colleges and universities faced new conditions, specifically the need for extensive expansion, for direct use of the bookstacks, and for new kinds of study facilities. To meet these conditions a new type of library structure — the so-called modular building — came into general use.

These modular buildings, although they sometimes lacked the traditional aesthetic qualities of the fixed-function buildings, have served the needs of the academic community very well indeed. That is, they have been capable of supporting, at a high quality level, library programs and activities that are now in existence; and it appears that they can support those that may come into existence if some of the early developments of the electronic communication revolution prove to be viable and acceptable to readers.

The history of the failure of the fixed-function library building and its replacement by the modular building need not be repeated in this account; but to establish a basis for communication, the essential differences between the two types of buildings will be briefly stated.

In the fixed-function library building (Columbia University — Butler Library; the central libraries of the Universities of Illinois, Michigan, and California at Berkeley), each part of the building was designed both in size and nature to house one specific library activity or function and was not easily adaptable to housing other kinds of activities. The multi-tier bookstacks with their 7-foot,

2-inch ceiling heights and stack columns on a 3-by-4½-foot base
could not be used as reading rooms or for staff activities because
of the low ceiling heights and the presence of columns. The handsome reading rooms, each designed as an architectural gem in
its own right with 20-30-foot ceilings, could not be divided
readily into small group study rooms, seminars, staff offices, or
library work rooms housing noisy machines, nor could they be
used economically to house books. Massive architectural stairways
and thick, weight-bearing walls gave the buildings a rigidity that
blocked efforts to change the internal relationships without excessive costs. Even with such changes, results achieved were often
not applicable to the mood of later times. Since each element
in the fixed-function library was limited in size to serve someone's
estimate of the institution's requirements at a given time, errors
in estimation or changes in the institution's needs could not be
corrected. And since the time of World War II the university,
particularly, has changed radically not only in size but in the kinds
of research and teaching programs it follows and in its concepts
of teaching methods.

These fixed-function buildings assumed a separation of readers
and the book collection, but since the middle thirties enlightened
educators (including librarians) have wanted readers to work in
the midst of book collections. By handling many books directly,
and thus comparing one book with another, a student might more
easily develop sound standards of evaluation than if he were
required to approach the collections through card catalogs, bibliographies, and circulation desk services.

In some universities the book collections grew faster, pro-
portionately, than did the enrollment, and vice versa. The fixed-
function building could not accommodate itself to these changes,
nor could it be enlarged efficiently to house the tremendous and
totally unexpected growth in both book collections and enroll-
ments that have occurred since the thirties.

The older and larger universities frequently could not abandon
their massive fixed-function buildings and have had to devise other
ways of solving their library problems. But on hundreds of campuses — especially new ones — a new type of library structure
began to evolve in the thirties.

The kind of building we call "modular" is nothing more than
the loft building structure brought up to date by artificial lighting

and ventilation. Angus Macdonald and Alfred Githens were responsible for developing the concept. Princeton, Iowa, North Dakota State, and Hardin-Simmons were the first institutions to use this plan in building new buildings. Since the 1940's there have been several hundreds of these buildings built in the United States, Canada, and Europe.

The essence of the modular library is simply that all of the floor space — except that occupied by fixed-core elements such as stair-wells, toilets, elevators, and special rooms — can be used to house any kind of library activity and that these activities can be moved and rearranged without involving structural changes in the library building.

The first real test of the adaptability of the modular library occurred in the University of Iowa library building in 1953, two years after it was built. Some new concepts of service for undergraduates were tried in the first unit of the building and some of these had to be abandoned because they were unsuccessful. Movable partitions and bookshelves were moved quickly, quietly, and inexpensively during the summer session in order to change the service concepts. Because the university lacked money to finish the first unit of the building, the finished ceiling was omitted and air cooling was left out. Robertson steel paneling was used as an exterior wall material on part of the structure. It lacked beauty in the traditional sense but even in the beginning it functioned well except for the lack of air cooling. Later, as money became available, the building was furnished properly and enlarged several times. The latest unit in 1971 will complete the structure as it was originally planned. The larger it becomes the better it functions. Many changes in interior arrangements have been made since the time the building was opened in 1951.

No one ever claimed that the exterior appearance of the Iowa library building was interesting or even good. Nor would one find much architectural excellence within it. There is nothing in the building that calls attention to itself as a thing of beauty. The building's beauty consists in its use by readers and in its high ratio of functioning to non-functioning space as a library.

This concept was and is offensive to some who take a different view about architectural beauty. Since the time of the Iowa building, architects have done many modular buildings that are just as functional as the Iowa building but endowed with qualities of beauty of a conventional nature. Washington University in St. Louis, still regarded as one of the very best medium-sized university libraries in the United States, was the first example of this; but now their number is legion.

There are several reasons why since World War II we have been getting a generation of buildings that are good.

The literature of academic library planning is now extensive and readily available; there are plenty of competent planning consultants available; the country is full of accredited and able architects; there are good examples in existing buildings to follow; and the bad buildings are generally known as such in the profession. Thus there is no reason why every college and university library building built in the last five years should not have been nearly perfect, at least from the point of view of functioning. As for the beauty in these buildings, even if everyone could agree on what is beautiful, architects can be expected to differ widely in their ability to create it. They should not be criticized for their inability to make every building equally beautiful in the eyes of all beholders, but they can be criticized for creating buildings that function less than perfectly.

It is the intent of this book to show the many ways architects have found to provide variety and interest in the modular buildings.

It is the author's conclusion that mistakes that have been made in the new library buildings resulted from one or a combination of several of the following situations:

1. The librarian was unable to write a complete and satisfactory library program. This means that he was not able to tell the architect clearly what the library is for, how it is to be used, and how the various parts are to interrelate. Sometimes the problem is that the librarian has been too proud to admit that he could not do this and unwilling to call in a consultant to help with the development of an enlightened program, even when he knew he could not do it himself.

2. The architect was unwilling to follow the program. This is occasionally a matter of lack of ability, but more often it appears to be sheer arrogance or willfulness.

3. The librarian and the consultant were not allowed to analyze and criticize the architect's work at each stage of its development.

4. Someone in the college or university administration (usually the President) imposed his views (which are usually uninformed) on the program or the architect's work.

5. The donor insisted on a monumental architectural expression that hampered the freedom of the architect to develop a functional building.

6. A faculty planning committee was allowed to control the program. This has almost always produced a building that was out of date and full of classical errors.

7. The campus planning office, with its own staff of architects, sometimes has interfered with the project architect unjustifiably.

8. In a few states the state building authority imposed regulations, concepts, and formulas of the kind that make it difficult for an architect to do a good building.

9. Insufficient funds sometimes forced planners to lower the quality of their building below levels they would otherwise hope to achieve.

10. Occasionally a difficult site problem forced decisions that were wrong.

11. Failure on the part of everyone involved to understand the significance or relevance of changes or forces taking place in society that affect the nature of library activities. Such people have not always seen that these changes make it mandatory that a library building be capable of adapting itself to housing new concepts of service and new capacities. Some of these forces are:

a. The growth in the numbers of carriers of information a library must acquire. Much has been said in recent years about the knowledge explosion, which has had the effect of doubling the size of library collections every ten to fifteen years. But in view of the complexity of the problems society now realizes it must solve if it is to survive, it should be clear that much more research and development will have to be supported if we are to solve these problems. This will result in an even greater flood of information carriers a university library must acquire, even though we hope new communication technology may cut down to some extent on the bulk of the carriers. Also, far on the horizon lies the fact that sometime in the future scholars in the now "emerging" nations of the world will be contributing to the reservoir of man's knowledge, and therefore to the numbers of books a library must acquire.

b. The new communications technology (see the report published by Educational Facilities Laboratories, Inc. on the effect of technology on library buildings.) No one can be certain at this time as to the effect the new developments will have on the *amount* of space a library will need, but we do know something about the effect these will have on the *nature* of the space. Technology that could reduce the amount of space needed for new publications (i.e. the computer) would not appear to have much effect in the near future. Technology that would reduce space needs for older books (i.e. microforms) seems to be concerned with making available materials that supplement rather than replace existing materials. All new technological developments seem to require more space for people using them than does the printed book.

    c. Changes in the composition of the campus and in enrollment patterns. It is impossible to predict today the pattern that will evolve in the next decade because so many conflicting forces are operating. We do know that more people will have to get more education than they are now getting but we do not know whether the increased number will be on the university campuses, in community colleges, or in vocational schools, or indeed on any campus. We do not know how soon, or to what extent, television will be used for formal teaching or what effect this will have on enrollments on campuses. We do not know if the large university is to be broken down into a larger number of smaller campuses, although current developments would suggest this. We do not know what is to happen to the traditional liberal arts concept of education in competition with curricula that are either interdisciplinary or "relevant."

    Thus, although it is clear that the future is most unclear, the moral for architects is entirely clear. Namely, libraries should be placed on sites that will permit indefinite expansion; and library buildings should be fully adaptable and capable of housing changing library programs and possibly of absorbing non-library activities.

    d. Emphasis on independent study seems to be the outcome of most of the good changes and improvements in teaching methods at all levels of education, but particularly at the high school and college levels. This affects not only the amount of library space needed, but also its nature.

    e. New interdisciplinary types of teaching and research programs, replacing the traditional single subject department, have already shown the need for a comparable difference in the structuring of library service. All signs point to more, rather than less, of these new interdisciplinary programs.

    f. Information science is creating a need for library subject specialists who are capable of entering into book selecting and reference work of a highly systematic nature as well as offering the kind of current awareness services private businesses and industries provide for their staffs. Librarians will need working quarters and access to hardware that were not required in the past. This calls for re-thinking the nature of library staff working space.

In short, a satisfactory library building should be thought of as a kind of growing organism capable of adapting itself to rapidly changing conditions.

To repeat, it was the inability of the fixed-function library buildings built prior to World War II (Northwestern University, Washington University, Fisk University) to provide new ratios between books and reader spaces, new kinds of reader stations facilities, and new staff quarters and relationships, as well as their inability to retain unity of service when enlarged, that made them obsolete. And it has been the ability, on the other hand, of the modular buildings erected since 1946 to adapt themselves to new conditions as well as to new size dimensions that has led to their widespread use.

Although most of the new buildings avoid the mistakes of the fixed-function buildings, there are certain types of mistakes now being incorporated in some new buildings that would appear to create the same difficulties in the new buildings that they created in the old ones. These might be categorized as follows:

1. Atriums and monumental stairways located in such a manner and of such a size that they lengthened unnecessarily the distance a reader must walk to get to the materials he wishes to use.

2. Massing the building on such an extensive dispersed basis that a reader's time is wasted, books are hard to locate, efficient organizations of the library services are difficult to arrange, and systematic enlargement of the building is impossible. For example, planning a building with departmental reading rooms of a fixed size with limited shelving means that when the shelves are full one book must be removed for each new book added. In the humanities, this would drive faculty members up the wall.

3. Use of floor to ceiling dimensions and ceiling designs that limit the adaptability of a library floor plan.

4. Use of light fixtures and systems that are ornamental rather than functional to the extent they do not provide good lighting.

5. Use of ceiling construction systems that will not permit the

containment of sound when new rooms have to be erected.

6. The use of towers that cannot be enlarged and are not large enough to house any one entire library department or activity.

7. Failure to meet the needs of paraplegics and the physically handicapped.

As this report will demonstrate, it is not necessary to repeat these errors to achieve interesting and beautiful buildings. Outstanding examples of successful binding of good functioning and beauty can be seen in the following buildings: Washington University in St. Louis, the University of Chicago, the University of Northern Iowa, Pacific Lutheran University, Indiana University, Arizona State University, Tulane University, the University of Tampa, Beloit College, Luther College, Amherst College, Southern Oregon College, Abilene (Texas) Christian College, and Georgetown University in Washington, D.C., to mention only a few located in various parts of the country.

Academic institutions differ from one another so widely in nature and purpose that the wide variety of architectural expressions portrayed in this report is inevitable. There is even a place on the American academic scene for a library building that is designed primarily as a work of art to satisfy the desires of a donor, a client, or even an architect, provided that all of these parties understand that the library is inside the building and that the welfare of the library is not of secondary importance. The great Gothic cathedrals may no longer house a significant religious activity, but they continue to give pleasure to tourists and they are important to students of the history of civilization.

Finally, there is one aspect of the nature of a library building that sometimes has presented puzzling hazards to the architect, and this is the fact that librarians differ considerably in their conceptions of how libraries should be operated and how library services should be organized. There is no one right way to organize a library.

It is for this reason that successful buildings have usually started with written building programs stating clearly and fully the concept of organization and service the librarian had in mind.

The architect, in turn, has needed the right to change the program when it was so restrictive it could not accommodate other programs in the future. This applies particularly to the layout of services on the main floor and to such matters as open versus closed access to books and the use of various media. An exception to this statement has to be made for library buildings designed for one specific function with no possibility that the function could change. Examples of such buildings are: a rare book library (Beinecke at Yale, or Lilly at Indiana); a storage library (the Center for Research Libraries in Chicago, or the storage library at Princeton); or, a college or undergraduate library as part of a university library complex (Indiana University, Lamont at Harvard University, the undergraduate library at Michigan, or the undergraduate library at the University of California at La Jolla and Berkeley.)

The New Gothic, University of Chicago

III

The Shape of Things

A. ON THE OUTSIDE

PRIOR to World War II architects had little choice in developing their library designs. They were expected to use one of the traditional classical forms — Greek or Roman temple, Gothic cathedral, Romanesque church, or colonial public building — for academic buildings. Typical examples: Deering Library at Northwestern, the law library at Columbia, Wilson Library at North Carolina, the University of Michigan, and the University of Illinois.

Today, architects have pretty much broken away from the traditional styles and have tried to design buildings that express not only the central role of knowledge but also the ways in which libraries are used. Only a few of the new buildings use traditional styles — except when they are additions to older buildings with a strong expression. For example:

North Carolina, Elan College. A mild southern colonial touch.

Tennessee Scarritt
College. Collegiate gothic
in style.

But in their efforts to develop new and interesting exterior designs for libraries, architects have found no single answer to the question of what a library should look like. Should it express the housing of books? Readers working in a variety of conditions? Librarians doing librarians' work? Faculty members working with students in the presence of books? The new electronic learning systems? As the study will show, there is much variety not only in the massing of buildings, but in their materials, decorative elements, and styles.

Some of the issues architects have had to cope with in determining the style and shape of a building are as follows:

A. The nature of the site and the character of adjacent buildings. The site is a determining factor mostly when it is sufficiently sloping to permit a main entrance at the top level, as at Tufts:

Massachusetts, Tufts University. Main entrance at top level. Two levels below.

Massachusetts, Tufts University. Top level entrance permits use of skylights without lessening efficiency of layout. View is from rear of main level looking toward entrance. Circulation desk on right side. Stairwell to lower levels on left.

or when it suggests the advisability of a below-ground library, as at the University of Illinois undergraduate library, or the University of Oregon Science Library, or Hendrix College:

Oregon, University of Oregon, Science Library. The new science buildings, forming L-shaped borders, suggested the possibility of an underground library.

Illinois, University of Illinois Undergraduate Library. The central mall had to be kept open. An underground library was the obvious answer. The two structures are the entrances. The central atrium is between the structures.

or when highly limited space dictates a high-rise type of building.

The use of a very tall tower at the University of Massachusetts was the result not of the site requirement but of the architect's wishes.

Rhode Island, Brown University, Science Library. Limited site called for highrise building.

California, California Institute of Technology. A tall, slender building placed in the center of an H-shaped campus.

Massachusetts, University of Massachusetts Library. A twenty-story tower on a broad platform.

The problem of achieving harmony with adjacent buildings has been handled by attempting to achieve resemblance and by direct contrast.

North Carolina, Duke University. An example of modified Gothic addition used with a strong Gothic structure.

Other architects have ignored the design of adjacent buildings, or of the parent building, when an addition is planned, and have achieved harmony by direct contrast.

Missouri, Washington University. On one side is a traditional Gothic church; on the other a modified Gothic structure, as shown. Photo by Herb Weitman, St. Louis, Missouri.

Georgia, Georgia Institute of Technology. A large and tall addition in two phases.

Connecticut, Yale University, Beinecke Library. Surrounded by Gothic structures.

New York, Cornell
University. The new and the
old have nothing in com-
mon — architecturally.

Illinois, Northwestern University. Skidmore, Owens
and Merrill designed a library contrasting sharply
with the old Gothic library.
The two are joined with a
simple passageway.

Illinois, University of
Chicago. The new Chicago
library (rear) in a traditional Gothic campus.

None of the campuses visited made the mistake of planning the library building at the center of the academic campus rather than along the edge of the center. Libraries placed along the edge can operate with only one entrance-exit whereas this is difficult if the library is in the middle. Multiple entrances-exits are expensive to staff and take up valuable space on the entrance level.

B. The massing of the building. The closer the massing approaches a globe or cube the more space each dollar will buy. Also, because a library operates with a high degree of interaction among its various departments, the more compact the building is the less time staff and readers have to spend doing their work. So, in terms of cost and efficiency the ideal massing for a library would be a cube or a rectangular shaped building with three-by-five dimensions. The more the building is stretched, the less efficient it becomes. However, the world would be a dull place if all buildings were plain cubes. Architects have tried to achieve variety and interest in many ways and by using many shapes. Such a variety of shapes might be classified as the following types:

1. *Cylinders or globes*. Not used extensively because of difficulty in expansion. Appropriate in libraries where the book collection and reader population can be held constant — such as a community college or an undergraduate library.

2. *Rectangular or square shapes*. With plain or highly decorative walls. Sometimes with extrusions and intrusions, large or small; very small to large "blockbuster buildings."

3. *Horseshoe shaped buildings*, with large front atriums.

4. *Cubes, globes, or towers placed on top of broad platforms.*

5. *Peripheral, or hole-in-the-head, buildings* with atriums of many shapes and sizes.

6. *Rorschach or inkspot buildings*. A kind of architectural happening.

7. *The double helix structures*. Linked hexagons or square boxes.

8. *Layer cake buildings*. Usually modular with heavy emphasis on horizontal lines.

9. *Underground libraries*. Modular moles.

Arizona, Arizona State University, Tempe. Carefully designed with Arizona's sunlight in mind. Type 2.

California, University of California at Berkeley, Undergraduate Library. Type 8. Setbacks at one end permit use of outdoor balconies. A modular building, efficient and appropriate to its setting. Has outdoor court at lower end.

California, University of, San Diego. Type 4. Diamond shaped box on a broad platform. Spectacular at night when venetian blinds are not drawn. Expansion possible only in platform.

California, San Diego State College. Type 2. A large square building, with no attempt to disguise its size. Photograph by Photographic Services, Audio-Visual Department, San Diego State College.

California, Chabot College.
Type 1. Round buildings like
this one are difficult to expand and thus are limited in
usefulness.

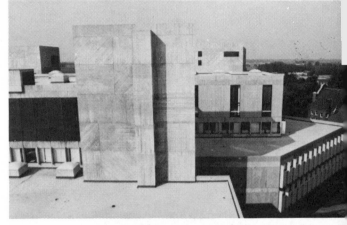

Canada, Guelph University.
Type 2 or 6. A square building with many small towers,
setbacks and extrusions at
lower level. Rugged exterior
does attract attention.

Canada, University of
Waterloo. Type 4. Large
square tower on wide platform. Good fenestration.
Ground level recessed.

Colorado, Southern Colo-
rado State College. Type 4.
Photo by Rush J. McCoy,
Golden, Colorado.

England, East Anglia University. Types 2 and 8. British cement. Square building with glass walls. A modular building. Very functional.

England, Exeter University. Central bookstack and reading areas. Type 2.

England, Essex University. Type 2. Block building with much use of glass walls. When partially open, draperies affect exterior looks of building.

England, Kent University. Type 2. Much variety in exterior wall surfaces — glass, cement, beams, and brick walls. See photo in stairwell section.

England, Warwick University. Type 2 or 5. This is a spartan exterior for a modular building.

England, York University. Type 2. Square building with glass walls. Large atrium filled with central stairway.

Florida, Florida Southern College. Type 2. A sculptured block, Stonehenge feeling. Few windows, much visual interest.

Florida, Florida Technical University. Type 2. A massive expression with sharply contrasted vertical and horizontal lines.

Florida, University of Florida Law Library. Type 2. Use of exterior wall panels to control sunshine.

Florida, University of Tampa. Type 2. Square building with a moorish design above entrance. Good fenestration.

France, University of Aix-en-Provence, Droit (Social Sciences). Type 8. Beyond the colonade a unit includes staff offices, the director's office, and other non-public functions. Central courtyard.

France, University of Aix-en-Provence, Letters. Type 2. Large square building with strong vertical lines.

France, Caen University.
Type 4. Tall stack tower in
center. Reading rooms and
staff at lower levels.

France, University of Lyon
Central Library. Type 2.
Entrance level much re-
stricted. A square building.

France, University of
Marseille, Droit Library.
Type 2. Large three story
building above ground.
Unusual stairway entrance.
Most new French libraries
have large central atriums.

France, University of
Marseille, Lumminy Library.
Type 8. A three-story science
building with horizontal lines.

France, University of Nice,
Humanities Division. Type 7.
Makes good use of side hill
site. Reading rooms on
several levels.

France, University of Nice, Science Library. Type 2. Follows contours of a cliff. Actually a rectangular building, fits setting beautifully.

France, Orsay University. Type 2. Stack block in center. Reader and staff facilities in adjacent units.

Georgia. Emory University. Type 4. Tall tower on a broad platform. Building set on edge of ravine with bridge connecting it with old library.

Germany, Aachen Technical
University. Type 8. Building
was under construction. A
modular building.

Germany, Bonn University.
Type 2. Tall stack tower in
rear. Low reading room
floors in front.

Germany, University of
Frankfurt. Type 4 or 6. Staff
and reader facilities in front
structure. First unit of stack
tower behind.

Germany, Stuttgart University. Type 2. A glass walled building. One of few continental libraries allowing direct access to bookstacks.

Idaho, University of Idaho. Type 2. Two intersecting boxes. Not sensational but pleasing in appearance as a result of good balancing of masses.

Illinois, University of Illinois Undergraduate. Type 9. An underground library with large atriums in center. The atrium walls are the library's exterior walls.

Illinois, Northwestern University. Type 7. Use of a cluster of hexagons. Each pod (or tower) contains one or more subject collections.

Indiana, Indiana University.
Type 4. Two boxes on a plat-
form. Photo by Eggers and
Higgins, Architects.

Indiana, Notre Dame Uni-
versity. Type 4. Tower is
sufficiently wide to meet
space needs for a long
time to come.

Iowa, Grinnell College.
Type 2. Glass walls facing
the highway on south side.
Dramatic at night. After-
noon sun creates problems.
Photo by Baltazar Korab.

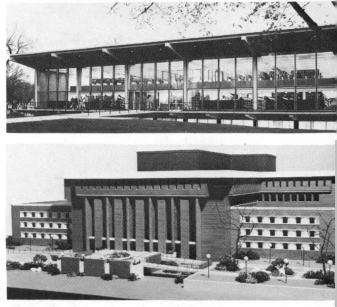

Iowa, University of Iowa.
Type 2. The final structure,
as shown, now being com-
pleted. An interesting building for many reasons; during
three stages of completion
metal knockout walls were
used and were not beautiful.

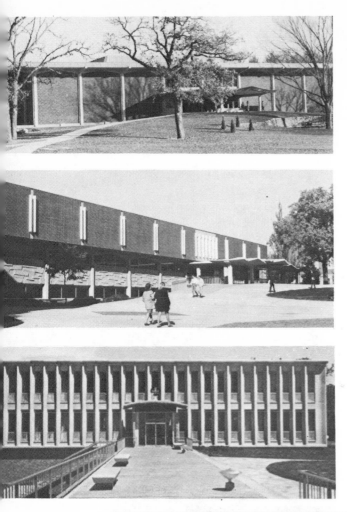

Iowa, Luther College. Type 2. A small square building, windowless on three sides. Impressive and dignified. One of the fine buildings in the United States.

Iowa, University of Northern Iowa. Type 2. One of the ten best buildings in the United States. Simple but appropriate design with good solution to fenestration problems. Excellent interior planning.

Kansas, Mt. St. Scholastica College, Atchison. Type 2. A rectangular, small college library. This building is beautifully sculptured.

Louisiana, Tulane University. Type 2. A square building with good fenestration. Ground level recessed along front of building.

Maryland, Johns Hopkins University. Type 9. Largely underground. Top level entrance.

Massachusetts, Clark University. Type 2 with units. Basically a square building with much irregularity in exterior walls. Central stack with reader facilities along edges.

Massachusetts, Hampshire College. Does not fit any of the nine types. Carefully designed to house functions not usual in a library. Not to be evaluated in traditional terms.

Massachusetts, Harvard University, Countway Medical Center. Type 5. Large square building with large central atrium.

Massachusetts, Harvard
University, Radcliffe. Types
3 and 5. Square building
with large atrium. Side view.

Massachusetts, Radcliffe
College. Types 3 and 5. The
central atrium forces readers
to do much walking. Has
interesting study spaces
of several kinds. Front view.

Massachusetts, Tufts Uni-
versity. Types 2 and 3. Top
level entrance as shown.
Study carrel pods on left.

Michigan, Eastern Michigan
University, Ypsilanti. Type
2. A square box with little
adornment. An example of
straightout, functional.

Michigan, Grand Valley
State College. Type 2. A
square box with variety in
its fenestration and exterior
stairways and massing.

Michigan, Michigan Tech-
nological University. Type
2. A square building with
somewhat classical treat-
ment of exterior walls.
Recessed ground level.

Minnesota, University of
Minnesota. Type 2. A large
research library — "blockbuster" as some architects
say. Carefully thought out
interior with lower level
connections to other
adjacent buildings.

Missouri, Stephens College.
Type 2. A small, rectangular
college library. A restrained
expression.

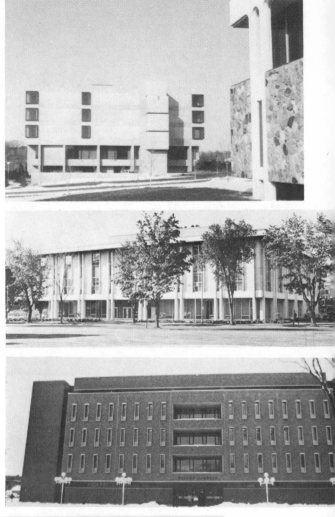

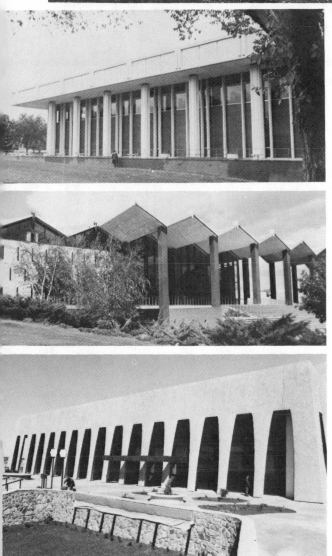

Missouri, Washington University, St. Louis. Type 2. Regarded by librarians as one of the great buildings. Was the first modular library to successfully weld "function" and "beauty." Photo by Hedrich Blessing.

Nebraska, University of Nebraska, Home Economics. Type 2. A square building with top floor overhang. Glass walls masked at lower levels to prevent glare.

Nevada, University of Nevada. Front view. Note slit type windows.

New Mexico, College of Santa Fe. Type 2. Square building with simple but appropriate exterior. Recessed western exposure to prevent glare.

New York, Hofstra University. Type 4. Tall tower on top of broad base.

New York, State University of New York, Albany. Type 3. A large front atrium creates a horseshoe shaped building. Forms part of a tightly coordinated campus plan.

New York, Wells College. Type 6. The building oozes down the hillside site.

Ohio, Bowling Green University. Type 4. Tall tower (with good fenestration) on large platform.

Ohio, Findlay College. Type 2. A simple, well designed small college library. Easily expanded.

Ohio, John Carroll University. Type 2. Square, with entrance on middle level.

Oklahoma, Oklahoma Christian University. Type 2. Library on ground level. Study carrels, etc. on top floor.

Oregon, Lewis & Clark College. A mild type 6 building. A dispersed structure appropriate to woodsy setting.

Oregon, Portland State College. Type 2. Wall panels can easily be removed and the building enlarged. A square building.

Oregon, Southern Oregon College. Type 2. Sits well on the side hill. Central entrance. Square building.

Pennsylvania, Beaver College. Small square building with simple exterior. Can be enlarged along side. Photo by Joseph Marchetti.

Pennsylvania, Bryn Mawr College. Type 2. Square buildings with massive front wall. Large atrium at one end.

Pennsylvania, Kutztown State College. Type 2. Can be enlarged vertically. Simple, square, inexpensive structure.

Pennsylvania, Lafayette College. Type 2. Simple, unadorned square building with slit windows.

Pennsylvania, Lehigh University, Sciences. Type 2. Built for vertical expansion. Square functional building with good fenestration.

Poland, Krakow University. The first real modular building in Northern Europe. Rectangular with glass walls.

Rhode Island, Providence College. Type 2 or 8. Square, small college library with strong horizontal lines.

Scotland, Edinburgh University. Type 2 or 8. Rectangular, with horizontal lines. A courageous design.

Scotland, Glasgow University. Type 2. Uses towers on edges for services. Matches surrounding buildings in most interesting way. Square building, easily enlarged.

South Carolina, Clemson
University. Type 2 or 5.
Square building with simple
exterior. Large front atrium.

South Dakota, University
of South Dakota. Type 2.
Simple, square building.
Could be expanded on all
four sides if necessary.
Recessed street level was
good idea for severe climate.
Fenestration confined to one
area on two sides, with slit
windows. A purely functional
building.

Sweden, Chalmers Techni-
cal University. Type 7. Early
post-war building. Charm-
ing but too small. Three
linked structures. Interesting interior.

Tennessee, Fiske Univer-
sity. Type 2. Square building with top floor overhang.
A well designed library.

Texas, North Texas State University. Type 2. Large square building. Almost windowless. Services in corners. Easily enlarged.

Texas, University of Texas at El Paso. Type 2. An addition placed in front of old building and connected by a beautiful courtyard.

Texas, University of Texas Undergraduate. Type 2. Rectangular building is designed to handle large numbers of readers and limited book collections. Good fenestration.

Utah, Brigham Young University. Type 2. Large rectangular building with simple facade. Recessed street level.

Utah, University of Utah.
Types 2 and 5. Large square
building with large central
atrium. Good fenestration.

Wales, University of Northern Wales. Type 2. The addition does not follow style of
original building.

Washington, Eastern Wash-
ington State College. Types
2 and 3. A modest front
atrium. Simple and effective
facade.

Washington, Western Washington State University, Pullman. Type 2. Rectangular with simple facade. "Nature boy" now a campus figure much beloved. Building easily enlarged. One of the early modular buildings.

Washington, D.C., Georgetown University. Type 2. Square structure with highly irregular exterior towers, warts, etc. An interesting building.

Wisconsin, University of Wisconsin, Agriculture. Type 2. Heavy, massive front entrance.

B.   VARIETY IN INTERIOR DESIGN

The examples shown in the previous section offer convincing evidence that architects have found many ways of taking the Basic Box (modular, squarish, and highly functional) and making it interesting on the outside.

Likewise, the need to develop a high quality reading environment within the modular buildings has led architects to achieve variety not only by various furniture arrangements but also by the use of atriums, mezzanines, and courtyards — all familiar architectural forms. In the fixed function buildings atriums were needed to supply natural light over circulation desks and sometimes reading rooms by means of skylights. Courtyards were used to bring more ventilation and natural lighting to readers through windows than was supplied by the exterior walls of the building. Mezzanines were used to provide more bookstacks in high ceiling reading rooms than the wall shelving around the edges of these rooms could provide.

The introduction of artificial lighting and ventilation enabled architects to design efficient and compact "modular" or loft type libraries. Since these buildings lacked the physical environment of a traditional library, architects have used traditional architectural forms to make the new buildings familiar and acceptable to the public, and perhaps even to give the architect a chance to satisfy his feelings about interior design. It could be said that early designers of automobiles retained buggy whip holders and other trappings from the horse-drawn buggies for much the same reasons. Clearly the atriums, mezzanines, and courtyards are not needed to supply lighting and ventilation in the modular buildings. It is obvious that many of the new buildings get along very well without them. But there can be no objection to their use if they are needed for the reasons mentioned above as long as they do not interfere with the proper functioning of the library. If they are placed in the center of the library or if they are very large, they do force readers to walk around them and thus do interfere to some extent with the proper functioning of the buildings. Most architects have tried to keep them small or to place them along the edge of the library where they interfere as little as possible with the efficiency of the building.

Atriums, Mezzanines, and Courtyards

California, University of California at San Diego, Undergraduate Library. Large central atrium. As shown, building was used as a central library. Now has been reorganized as an undergraduate library.

California, Chabot College. A round building with mezzanines on two sides. Circulation desk in center on main level.

California, Stanford University, Undergraduate Library. Atrium in center of library is so large it wastes the time of readers and staff.

California, Westmont College. Places main stairwell in front atrium, thus making good use of the space.

Canada, Guelph University. Books below and research carrels above lounge-gallery on this side of the mezzanine.

Canada, Guelph University. On the opposite side of the mezzanine. Carrels and some bookstacks are located. Two of the carrels are for researchers — with lockers.

Colorado, Loretta Heights College. Good use of a front atrium. Circulation desk is within atrium. Camera was placed just inside front door of library.

England, Kent University. Books below. Rooms and carrels on mezzanine.

England, York University. Large central atrium. Placing the stairway within the atrium helps minimize a quite large hole in the center of the building.

Florida, University of Tampa. Placing the atrium at the end of the building enabled the architect to design a reading lounge area.

France, University of Aix-
en-Provence. Droit Library.
Pleasant courtyard separates
administration and staff
areas from reading rooms
and stacks.

France, University of Lyons.
Bookstacks on the mezza-
nine in this section of the library. Open wall.

France, University of
Marseille. The Lumminy
Library. Typical of new
French university library
buildings.

Georgia, Georgia Institute of Technology. Reading area on one side of mezzanine, staff rooms on the other.

Georgia, University of Georgia Law Library. Almost all law libraries have a mezzanine along one side.

Germany, University of Frankfurt. Current journals above, books below on small mezzanine in center of reading room.

Germany, Stuttgart University. An elegant courtyard along reading rooms.

Illinois, University of Chicago. A two-level central atrium between the second and third floors, designed to break monotony of large reading area.

Illinois, University of Illinois, Undergraduate Library. An underground library needs this kind of openness.

Illinois, University of Illinois, Undergraduate Library. The site problem dictated an underground building. The large central atrium seems logical, right, attractive.

Illinois, Northwestern University. An unusual atrium in the undergraduate part of the library.

Kansas, Mt. St. Scholastica College. Example of small front atrium. Note card catalog, charging desk, and front door at end of atrium — compact, efficient.

Maryland, Johns Hopkins
University. An underground
library with main entrance
on top level. Central atrium
and stairway bring light to
charging desk and card
catalog area.

Massachusetts, Amherst
College. A modest atrium in
center of library interferes
little with use of library.

Massachusetts, Clark Uni-
versity. Many different
shaped atriums separate
bookstacks from reading
areas, from the main floor to
the top. Bridges cross the
openings at appropriate
points.

Massachusetts, Harvard University, Countway Library. Two central atriums: oval shaped atrium from main floor to basement, and high atrium extending to roof, with carrel studies hung along one side.

Massachusetts, Harvard University, Countway Library. Along one wall of the central atrium the architect hung small study rooms — good places from which to pour hot lead on the enemy in case of invasion, but not good for study.

Missouri, Washington University. By planning the main stairway along one side of the front atrium and using the three other sides for library functions, the hole becomes an asset to the building. Beautiful as well as functional.

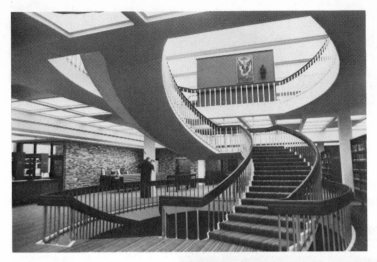

New Mexico, College of Santa Fe. By placing the curved stairway within the atrium near the front (see circulation desk on left), the architect created a dramatic effect and wasted little space.

New York, Wells College. This building is placed on a sloping site with many levels. This and the picture following show several kinds of balcony and mezzanine reading rooms.

New York, Wells College. Another view of the various levels in the building. Severe heat losses occur at lower levels.

North Carolina, University of North Carolina Undergraduate Library. A fairly large central atrium. Upholstered benches are much appreciated on a Monday morning.

Ohio, Bowling Green University. A small atrium in a large building, placed adjacent to central core (elevators, etc.) and thus an asset with little loss in efficiency.

Ohio, John Carroll University. A small, curved front atrium wastes little space and opens up a nice view.

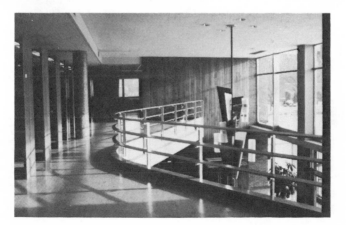

Ohio, Wooster College. A
large central atrium with
open stairway at one end.
On the second floor the
traffic has to flow around
the atrium.

Oregon, University of Oregon, Science Library. An
underground site adjacent to
the science quadrangle. The
central courtyard provides
light to readers placed
around it.

Oregon, Southern Oregon
College. A false atrium!
Creates effect without doing
any harm. The exit control
desk is directly under it.

Pennsylvania, Haverford College. A mezzanine was placed in the nave of a church connected to library use.

Pennsylvania, Haverford College. A view of the mez- zanine from the side opposite to previous view.

Pennsylvania, Lehigh Uni- versity, Science Library. A small atrium near the front door with main stairway within the atrium.

Pennsylvania, University
of Pennsylvania. This building uses central mezzanines
to permit impressive front
reading rooms.

Pennsylvania, University of
Pittsburgh. Atriums on
either side of the central
communication core force
readers to go around the
hole to get at books on the
intermediate level.

Scotland, Glasgow Univer-
sity. A series of small atriums
on alternate floor levels
breaks the regularity of the
eight-foot ceiling heights.

South Carolina, Clemson University. A massive front atrium uses a large amount of space in the building.

Texas, University of Texas at El Paso. Beautiful use of courtyard to join two quite different styles of buildings. This and the Washington University library are the two outstanding examples of courtyards. Photo by Darst-Ireland Photograph, El Paso, Texas.

Utah, University of Utah. A large atrium in the middle of the building. The main stair-way and elevators are placed between front door and atrium.

Wisconsin, Beloit College.
Atrium placed at rear of
building, beyond two-level
stack spine, provides lounge
area looking out over
wooded campus. Carrels
and books on the mezzanine.

Wisconsin, University of
Wisconsin, College of Agri-
cultural Library. A large
central atrium somewhat
larger than one module.
Note how architect worked
around the column.

Interior Atrium, University of Chicago

IV

Essential Functions
and Their
Physical Implications

To understand why the new academic library buildings included in this study tend to be pretty much alike in their interior arrangements, the following summary of library operations is given.

A. THE LOGIC OF THE MAIN FLOOR LAYOUT

College and university libraries may differ from one another considerably in the way they organize their facilities for reading and bookshelving; but they tend to follow similar concepts in designing their main floor for the following reasons.

Before a reader can find the book (or other carrier of information) or the information he needs, he must first find out which book has the information and, next, where this book is located. Libraries have extensive tools and services to assist the reader in these matters. These Keys or Locators to the library are located on the main floor where the reader can get at them quickly once he enters the building. The Keys include the following:

1. Bibliographies and indexes for all types of publications (books, periodicals, government documents, microforms, manuscripts, records, tapes, and audiovisual media) have been developed as indexes to the information in the world's reservoir of published information. Although people find the printed book and other media good sources from which to extract information, they frequently cannot remember later which book contained the information they extracted. Bibliographies and indexes become the memory to the

contents of the publications in such a manner that the inquirer
has a reasonable chance of finding the source of the information
he needs — provided he knows which bibliographies and indexes
to use and provided that he knows how to use them.

2. Catalogs. Once the reader discovers the names of the publications that contain the information he wants, he next must find
out where they are — if they are in the library in which he is
working. The library catalog, in either card or printed volume
form, tells him if the book he wants is owned by the library.
National library catalogs tell him which other libraries own the
book if his does not; the *Union List of Serials* tells him where
journals are located; and other location tools exist. The Interlibrary
Loan Department is designed to help him borrow materials from
other libraries.

3. The Reference Department, consisting of librarians and
books, both highly skilled and specialized in helping readers locate
information, is a necessity in every academic library. This may
be centralized to include all subject fields, or it may be decentralized
into various parts of the building with the specialized books and
staff located where the books for those subjects are located.

4. Current periodicals. The time gap between the discovery
of new information (or the completion of the manuscript of a piece
of creative writing) and the publication of this information in printed
book form is wide — sometimes a matter of years. The periodical
exists as a quick outlet for new information and for short bits of
writing that will never appear in book form. Scholars, especially
in the sciences, must examine closely the current periodicals in
their specialty to be sure they have the latest information.

5. Circulation records. The reader may not find the book he
wants on the shelf because someone else is using it, it has been
lost, sent to the bindery, or loaned to another library. Circulation
records are supposed to indicate where every book is when it
is not on the shelves.

These five departments or services constitute the Keys to the
library, and because they are the first part of the library a reader
uses as he enters and the last part he uses as he leaves, they
are located on the main floor of the library.

Other departments in the library demand special locations
because of the nature of their work or their use. For example:

Reserve book departments are usually the most heavily used

part of the library. For this reason they are located as near the entrance as possible, either as a part of the main circulation desks in smaller libraries or as a separate department one level below or above the main floor (street level).

Technical processes departments — acquisitions, cataloging, and serials — are usually located on the same level with the Keys because their staffs make frequent use of the Keys. Because space is limited on the main floor, especially in those libraries where the architect recessed the walls of this level, some libraries place the technical processes staffs on other levels with quick and direct elevator service to the main level. This causes some waste in staff time and isolates the staff in a manner that is objectionable to some librarians. Oral and visual communication links between the Keys and the technical processes staff can minimize both disadvantages of a distant location.

B. The Elements of the Main Floor Layout

As stated in the previous section, the bases for the arrangement of staff services and book materials on the main floor of an academic library have been determined by the ways readers approach the carriers of information, and by the way each library is organized to facilitate the approach. There is no one correct way of arranging the elements. For example, although all academic libraries place the card catalog and a reference department on the main floor, some decentralize the reference staffs and materials onto the various levels of the libraries. Likewise, some libraries place their technical processes staffs below or above the main floor. The following statements are intended to interpret the issues illustrated by the photographs and floor plans in this section.

1. The Entrance — Through the Storm Vestibule to the Lobby

Architectural Intent

1. To place a library directory where it can be seen immediately by visitors.

2. To channel traffic to the right side (most Americans are accustomed to "keep to the right") so that once visitors are in the lobby they will not cross the traffic lines of people leaving the building by the circulation and exit control desks.

3. To place, in the storm vestibule, access to activities (such

as cafes, cloak rooms, lockers, all night study rooms) whose users are not expected to pass by the exit control desks.

4. To place exhibit cases and displays where they can be readily seen.

5. To open up a view of the library elements the visitor will want to see first — circulation desk, card catalog, main stairway, reference department.

6. To enclose the noise-causing elements — circulation desk, stairway, elevators — so that their users do not disturb readers on the main floor.

Canada, Guelph University. As you enter the front door you see the exit control desk and information lobby beyond. To the left is the main stairway.

Canada, Guelph University. Inside the information/ circulation desk to the left is a lounge area and current periodicals beyond.

Canada, Guelph University. Inside the information area to the right is the card catalog and the reference collection.

Florida, University of Florida Law School. One of the few law libraries with circulation desk outside the reading room. Reserve books are behind counter. Entrance to reading rooms on left.

Georgia, Emory University. Almost all the street level is a lobby. Exit control on left. Main stairway to keys is below. Note umbrella stand.

Illinois, University of Chicago. Storm vestibule with main entrance on right. Entrance to all-night study room on left.

Indiana, Earlham College. Circulation desk on left. Stairs straight ahead. Card catalog and reference on right.

Iowa, University of Northern Iowa. Card catalog and circulation to left. Reference department ahead, beyond glass partition. Main stairway on right.

Massachusetts, Tufts University. Top floor entrance permits use of sky lights. From front door one sees stairway to lower levels, card catalog and reference department beyond. Circulation desk is left of front door.

Minnesota, University of Minnesota. A large building. Card catalog and escalator straight ahead.

Minnesota, University of Minnesota. Circulation to left of front door.

Minnesota, University of Minnesota. Reference to right of the front door.

New York, Cazenovia College. A convenient and compact plan for a small college. Photo taken from front door.

Ohio, Findlay College. Small library. Everything in sight. Glass wall between noisy elements and reading rooms.

Ohio, University of Northern Ohio. An attractive view from the front door. Circulation desk on left. Reference center straight ahead.

76

Oregon, Lewis & Clark University. Looking toward front door. Circulation desk on left. Exit control on right side. Card catalog and reference desk on either side.

Oregon, Portland State College. View from front door toward entrance gates, exit control desk, information desk, and circulation desk in rear.

Oregon, Southern Oregon College. Card catalog straight ahead. Reference to right. Circulation and reserve on left side. Note false atrium.

Pennsylvania, Temple University. Large, open entrance area with circulation desk and card catalog in rear. There is much room left for expansion of reference department on left side and card catalog on right. Ten-cent store light fixtures.

South Dakota, University of South Dakota. From the front door the circulation desk, card catalog, and reference desk are visible. Exit wall on left. Entrance on right side of vestibule.

Tennessee, Belmont College. Small building with pleasant view of card catalog, reference collection, current periodicals, from front door.

Texas, Southwestern University. Looking toward entrance from the fireplace, one sees entrance and exit control desk on the right, circulation desk and card catalog on the left, with reference collection opposite the circulation desk.

Texas, Southwestern University. Close-up of exit control desk and main stairway.

Texas, University of Texas, Undergraduate Library. Front lobby separates main circulation desk and stairway, on left, from reading room.

Utah, University of Utah. Beyond the storm vestibule is a large central atrium with circulation desk in rear, reference on left, reserve desk on right.

Wisconsin, Beloit College. The president wanted books to be in evidence. From front door, circulation desk is on left, books in center, reference on right, reading areas in rear.

Wisconsin, University of Wisconsin at Milwaukee. Circulation and reserve desks are to right. Reference and card catalog straight ahead, separated by glass wall from lobby. Handles large student body nicely.

Wyoming, University of Wyoming. An excellent layout. Entrance in center at rear. Stairway close by, circulation desk on right with reference department on left.

2. Exit Controls

Architectural Intent

1. To narrow traffic to a single lane so that the inspector can make certain the library materials are charged out.

2. To arrange facilities so that in slack periods the work can be done by the circulation desk attendant, in small libraries or, in larger systems, by one person, and in such a way that in busy periods more lines can be staffed.

3. To provide working surface so that readers can open their brief cases for inspection.

California, University of California, Berkeley, Undergraduate Library. Two lines of traffic possible. Only one exit line in use at most times. Turnstiles for in and out traffic.

California, University of California, San Diego. Has three sets of exit control desks like the one shown. Turnstile for entrance only.

Canada, University of
Waterloo. Single traffic line
controlled by turnstile.
Main stairway at left. Has
louverall ceiling lighting.

England, University of East
Anglia. Two lines possible
for both entrance and exit.
Turnstiles for in and out
lines.

England, University of Warwick. From front door, circulation desk is next to exit
control. Traffic on left side.

Idaho, University of Idaho.
Good arrangement using
end of circulation desk for
exit control.

Illinois, University of Chicago. Two lines possible, only one in use most of the time.

Indiana, University of Indiana. Electronic bell-controls at exit alert staff member when a student tries to outwit checkout procedures.

Iowa, University of Northern Iowa. End view of entrance/exit control. Circulation desk is beyond. Excellent layout for all entrance/exit control elements. Note location of card catalog and entrance to reference department and main stairway on right.

Massachusetts, Harvard University, Lamont Library. Note use of two exit lines with entrance between them. Entrance control on near side, exit far side.

Nebraska, University of Nebraska, Home Economics
Library. Single lines in and
out with entering line on
left side of desk.

Nevada, University of Ne-
vada. Entrance to left. Exit
at end of circulation desk.
Three lines in, one line out.

New Zealand, University of
Auckland. Two exit lines
possible at end of circulation
desk. Entrance on right.

Oregon, Portland State College. Two to four lines of
traffic possible. Entrance
turnstiles beyond card catalog on left.

Oregon, Southern Oregon College. Entrance on right. Exit on left side of counter. Could run two lines at rush hours. Circulation desk on left. Card catalog at far end Reference on right.

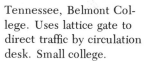

Pennsylvania, Lafayette College. A tight, small exit at end of circulation desk. Entrance lines at left of column.

Tennessee, Belmont College. Uses lattice gate to direct traffic by circulation desk. Small college.

Texas, Abilene Christian College. From the front door. Circulation desk on left; card catalog and reference on right. Exit control in foreground.

Texas, University of Texas,
Undergraduate Library. A
heavily used building. Several lines of traffic possible.
Main stairway at left.

Washington, Pacific Luth-
eran University. Exit turnstile at far end of circulation
desk. Note exhibit cases
near front of building.

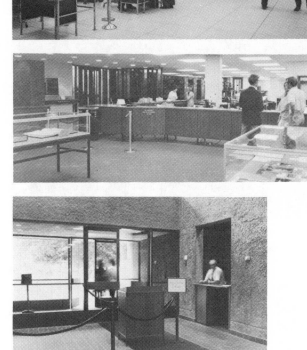

Washington, D.C., George-
town University. Office for
guard along edge. Second
guard sits at center desk
when needed. Theatre
ropes channel traffic.

Wisconsin, Beloit College.
Places the circulation desk
near door at left front. Stairwell visible on left.

3. Reference Departments

Architectural Intent

1. To make inquiry desk clearly visible from the entrance and to provide work offices for the staff near the inquiry desk or desks.

2. To place inquiry desk so that discussions there do not bother readers.

3. To make provisions for the comfort of inquirers who may need only a quick answer, or a long discussion with the reference librarians.

4. To place reference books on reference book ranges short enough so that readers do not have to carry reference books long distances.

5. If a central reference staff pool is the accepted system, to provide the following relationship between desk, staff rooms, and books.

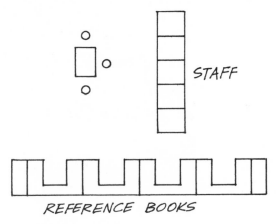

If staff is decentralized throughout the building, the same relationships are to be provided in the various areas.

6. To provide close spatial relationships with the card catalog. If the decentralized system is used, visual or electronic links are to be provided.

7. To facilitate the joint reference/acquisition work done by reference librarians. Closeness to the Acquisition Department is useful. Large offices (120 square feet) and flat table work space is to be provided for this work.

8. To provide a general information desk unless this function is provided elsewhere.

REFERENCE DEPARTMENTS — STAFF OFFICES

Arizona, Arizona State University. Long desk with reference books on low shelves.

California, University of California at Santa Cruz. Formal counter with staff is in rear.

California, Chabot College. A community college. U-shaped counter in middle of reading room.

Canada, University of Waterloo. Formal desks with books in rear.

England, East Anglia University. Desk in front, offices for reference staff (four) along edge of room.

Florida, University of Florida. Single desk with lounge chairs and table behind for extended talks.

Georgia, Emory University. Several desks in area adjacent to reference book area.

Illinois, University of Chicago. Example of decentralized reference bibliographic staff located on same floor as book collection in area of their specialization.

Illinois, University of Chicago. Another view with offices near subject bibliographies and reference tools.

Illinois, Northwestern University. Desks in front of work area for reference staff.

Illinois, Northwestern University. A special place for reference department staff to teach students use of library.

Indiana, Earlham College. One desk in front of two staff offices. Very good.

Iowa, University of Northern Iowa. Desk in front of series of offices. The best arranged department of its kind in the country.

Iowa, University of Northern Iowa. Interior of one of the reference staff offices.

Louisiana, Tulane University. Nice desks in front of offices. Each staff member has a table behind his desk with an office behind this.

Massachusetts, Amherst College. An unusual arrangement. Desk in front of office with peep hole window. OK for staff but embarrassing for student inquirer.

Massachusetts, Tufts University. Counter in front of office next to books.

Michigan, Central Michigan University. Small offices at head of reference collection.

Michigan, Grand Valley, State College. Desk — across corridor from office.

Michigan, Wayne State University Medical Library. Two desks with telephones out in open. A bit unusual to have phones in the open because of noise. Note light fixtures in ceiling bays.

Minnesota, University of Minnesota. Reference office pool behind counter.

Missouri, Washington University. From behind reference desk. Circulation desk on left. Reference office on right.

Oregon, Oregon State University. Reference offices behind desks.

Oregon, Portland State College. Divisional reference desks with work room behind. A very well planned layout. One for each floor.

New York, Cornell University. Reference desk in front of office. Those are bagels on a stick behind desk — not an inherent part of department.

Pennsylvania, University of Pennsylvania. Large counter near books.

Rhode Island, Brown University. Two desks near office. Behind partition is card catalog. A good layout.

Rhode Island, Brown University. In front of partition in preceding part are two reference desks near card catalog.

South Dakota, University of South Dakota. Desk where the action is. See next picture.

South Dakota, University of South Dakota. Behind reference desk is office for staff.

Tennessee, Vanderbilt University. Counter with desks behind and offices in rear. Note ease with which inquirer can go from counter to desk to office. Good layout.

Texas, University of Texas, Undergraduate Library. Desks are placed out where the students are.

Washington, Pacific Lutheran University. Desks at rear of card catalog area. Reference books beyond.

Washington, D.C., Georgetown University. Note offices for reference staff opposite desk across corridor.

Wisconsin, University of Wisconsin at Milwaukee. Open desks in front of reference department. Illustrates need for chairs.

Wyoming, University of Wyoming. General reference department office and desk. Note closeness to main circulation desk beyond partition.

REFERENCE DEPARTMENTS — SPECIAL SERVICES

Arizona, Arizona State University. Special information counter at entrance to reference department.

Arizona, Arizona State University. Use of special telephone.

Utah, University of Utah. Special desk to handle telephone inquiries at public catalog and reference. See next picture.

Utah, University of Utah. Telephone inquiry can be discussed at card catalog by means of tele-jacks in catalog cabinets and stand-up tables.

Reference Departments — Materials Housing

California, California Institute of Technology. A full divisional reference department — office, desk-catalog and collection.

California, California Institute of Technology. Low shelves at ends of ranges.

California, University of California at Los Angeles. Low shelving for printed library catalogs. High shelves for reference books.

California, University of California at Santa Cruz. Lazy Susan for National Union Catalog. Each level rotates. Not more than one user at a time for each shelf level.

Canada, University of Guelph. Blocks of reference books and carrels along edges. Rather long ranges for a reference collection.

Canada, University of Guelph. Index shelving.

France, University of Lyon. Books and tables. Ranges are about nine feet long.

Georgia, Emory University. High cases for regular reference. Note stand-up tables for card catalog and reference book use.

Idaho, University of Idaho.
Books on regular shelves
interspersed with tables and
low shelves on tables.

Illinois, University of Chicago. Low section at end of reference shelf ranges provides
place to use books.

Indiana, Earlham College.
Note inspection shelves at
end of reference ranges.

Iowa, University of Iowa. A U-shaped alcove of high book cases with low case in center.

Iowa, University of Iowa. A row of alcoves.

Maryland, Johns Hopkins University. Reference books between card catalog and bookstacks on main floor of library.

Maryland, Johns Hopkins
University. A divisional
reference collection.

Massachusetts, Amherst
College. Alternate low and
high cases for reference
books.

Michigan, Central Michi-
gan University. Combined
reference book case and
carrel in reference area.
Could also be used as
research carrel.

Michigan, Wayne State University, Medical Library. Al-
ternating high and low cases
for medical library.

Minnesota, University of Minnesota. Reference carrels behind cases for reference books.

Missouri, University of Missouri at Rolla. Both low and high cases in reference room.

Ohio, Northern Ohio University. Reference center. Tables and low cases in central area. Regular book collection behind. Note light fixtures at right angles to ranges.

Oregon, Oregon State University. Low cases.

Oregon, Oregon State University. Sloping tops used for most of reference collection. For stand-up use.

Pennsylvania, University of Pennsylvania. Reference books in both block and alcove arrangement.

Pennsylvania, University of Pittsburgh. Special cases for indexes.

Rhode Island, Brown University. Pull-out inspection shelves in reference department. Ties up space while reader stands in front of case, but is easy to use.

Scotland, Glasgow University. Reference books on wall cases with shelf for reading.

South Carolina, Clemson University. Reference books next to card catalog. Entrance is on right of card catalog. Note light fixture.

Texas, Abilene Christian College. Reading shelf in bookshelf range.

Texas, Abilene Christian College. Reference book ranges arranged at forty-five degree angle with reading shelves in each range.

Utah, University of Utah. Layout of reference book alcoves. There are four kinds of reading facilities.

Utah, University of Utah. Reference books with regular carrels between.

Utah, University of Utah.
Reference books and tables.

Utah, University of Utah.
Reference books and
counter.

Wisconsin, University
of Wisconsin at Milwaukee.
Alternate low and high
cases.

ATLAS CASES

Georgia, Emory University.
Atlas cases with sloping tops.

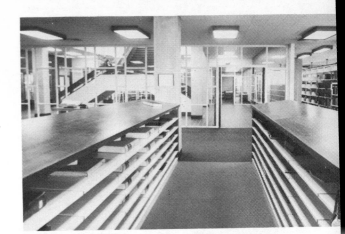

Massachusetts, Tufts University. Atlas cases.

Michigan, University of Michigan, Undergraduate Library. Regular cases with globe.

Missouri, Washington University. Special case with flat top.

Ohio, John Carroll University. Regular atlas cases at ends of bookstack ranges.

South Dakota, University of South Dakota. Low atlas case. Top used for reading.

INDEX CASES

California, California Institute of Technology. Tables with sloping shelf. The case is top heavy in appearance.

California, University of California at Los Angeles. Wall shelves and ledge for readers. Very convenient.

Indiana, Earlham College. Top of low case used for reading.

Iowa, University of Iowa.
Two shelves above sloping
ledge for reading.

Louisiana, Tulane University. Two shelves on tables.

Michigan, Eastern Michigan
University. Stand-up height
cases with stools.

Minnesota, University
of Minnesota. Stand-up
counter with shelves above.

Michigan, Grand Valley
State College. Two shelves
on tables. Stools.

Missouri, Washington Uni-
versity. Inspection shelf at
end of book case. Counter
on opposite wall.

Oregon, Portland State College. Table and two shelves.

Pennsylvania, University of
Pittsburgh. Custom cases.
Stool looks uncomfortable.

Texas, Rice University.
The right way to plan a wall
ledge.

Washington, Pacific Luth-
eran University. OK for
stand-up work but hard to
use with stool because there
is no place for legs.

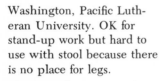

Wisconsin, University
of Wisconsin at Milwaukee.
Stand-up cases.

4. Serials — Background Information and Architectural Issues

Serials come to a library in a wide variety of formats: periodicals of varying sizes, monographs belonging to series, and newspapers. Libraries acquire most of these in unbound form in original format and may either bind them for permanent storage at the completion of each volume or purchase microforms, either discarding the originals or leaving them on the shelves.

Because serials contain the results of new research and scholarship, their prompt appearance on the shelves is important. Their handling, from the time of arrival until they are placed on the shelves, must be fast, efficient, and careful. The library's record of the presence of each issue of each title is usually kept on cards fastened flat in shingle fashion in special drawers. This record is consulted both by the staff and the public who need to know if a given serial is in the library.

The *architectural issues* for serials departments depend on administrative decisions on the following matters:

1. The handling system from time of arrival until the current issues are placed on the shelves. This involves placing tables in the mailing room upon which large sacks of mail can be dumped. Current issues must be unwrapped, stamped with ownership marks, alphabetized in bins, placed on book trucks, and sent to the check-in records. From there they go to the display shelves where they remain until each volume is completed. At that time they go to the bindery and then to serial catalogers for final cataloging.

2. The place and manner in which the current issues are to be placed for use. In libraries that have the space, the last issue is placed flat on a sloping shelf, with the rest of the issues of the last volume either in a bin behind the sloping shelf, or on a flat shelf under it. A single-faced three-foot shelving section will take three sloping shelves with five journals per shelf, or fifteen per section. Libraries lacking space for this kind of shelving usually place the current issues flat on shelves spaced closely together. Special cases in which the current issue can be shelved vertically are available, and various kinds of cabinets and bins are available.

For newspapers, current issues are fastened to rods and suspended in racks or folded once and placed flat on shelves. Two rather new systems have come into use: one places the once-folded paper on a sloping shelf, holding it in place by a hinged plastic cover, the other suspends the current issues in a canvas hammock hung from horizontal rods.

Reading areas for serials usually contain a variety of reader stations — lounge-type furniture, tables, and carrels for note taking. The reader may want to use his typewriter for this purpose or he may take the journal to a photocopier, which is now an essential part of a serials reading room.

Since most libraries store some of their serials in microform, provisions for their storage and use will be necessary in the serials reading room, unless the library centralizes microforms in one room. Reader printer machines will be needed. (See Chapter VI, C., Microforms — Housing and Use, for facility requirements.)

The problem of keeping current issues available for use is a serious one. This may require a special closed-access area where issues are charged out over a charging desk, or one area from which issues may not be taken. Losses from theft are heavy in most libraries. Use of one of the electronic theft preventors is limited because of the cost of using it on each issue.

Indiana, Indiana University. Behind counter, the serials check-in records.

Indiana, Indiana University. Serials control desk.

Indiana, Indiana University. Serials work room behind counter.

Indiana, Indiana University. Serials unpacking and bindery preparation.

Indiana, Indiana University. Serials preparation.

Indiana, Indiana University. Serials cataloging.

Iowa, University of Northern Iowa. Public entrance to
serials records.

Iowa, University of Northern Iowa. Doors at ends of
room leading to technical
processes area are locked at
night but public door is kept
unlocked so a reader can
always consult the records.

5. Current Periodicals and Newspapers

CURRENT PERIODICALS

Arizona, University of Arizona, Science Library. Current issues in pamphlet
boxes.

California, California Institute of Technology. Current issues above and back issues below.

California, University of California at San Diego. Current serials on sloping shelves in alcoves.

California, University of California at Santa Barbara. Large collection. Issues kept flat on shelves.

California, University
of California at Santa Cruz.
Magazines shelved flat with
lounge chairs and carrels
along wall of courtyard, in
background.

California, University
of California at Santa Cruz.
Shows carrels next to courtyard.

California, Chabot College.
Serpentine line of ranges
holding current issues.

California, Stanford University, Undergraduate Li-
brary. Another grouping for
lounge and table use.

Colorado, Loretta Heights College. A special type of shelf. Tables placed among ranges.

Canada, University of Guelph. Alternate rows of high and low shelves, the latter used for indexes.

Canada, University of Guelph. A second type of shelving in reading room.

Delaware, University of Delaware. Indexes shelved near current issues, which are shelved flat.

England, East Anglia University. Series of cases, current issues on top, back issues below. Here lounge furniture is between cases with tables on side.

England, Essex University. Low cases for current issues.

England, Keele University. Current issues on front of cupboard doors. Back issues on shelves in the cupboards.

England, Kent University. Cupboard doors for current issues. Back issues behind.

England, University of Warwick. Flat shelving with indexes on low range. Tops used for reading. Tables to the left.

France, Aix-en-Provence
University, Letters Library.
Low cases with sloping
fronts.

France, Nice University,
Science Library. Low cases
with sloping fronts.

France, University of Lyon.
Current issues placed vertically behind glass front.

Germany, Frankfurt Uni-
versity. Bottom two shelves
of racks slope. Other shelves
with glass fronts hold journal
issues vertically. Note ventilation outlets.

Germany, Giessen University. A-frame cases with current issues held vertically.

Germany, Stuttgart University. High cases with sloping shelves. Back issues kept elsewhere.

Holland, Delft Technological University. Overhead racks. Each shelf sloped to hold the issues.

Georgia, Emory University. Pleasant lounge area next to current issues.

Illinois, University of Illinois, Undergraduate Library. Low cases in a browsing room atmosphere.

New York, Wells College. Indexes near current issues. Note fixed location stools and cases. This is not usually done because of difficulty of moving cases.

North Carolina, Duke University. Ranges in blocks, distributed around a reading room.

Ohio, John Carroll University. Current issues are kept near serials offices just beyond. Desk for serials librarian is in sight.

Ohio, Ohio Northern University. Attractive reading area near current journals.

Michigan, Grand Valley College. A compact block of ranges with serials librarian close by.

Michigan, Wayne University Medical Library. Contains "last week's" current issues of journals.

Minnesota, University of Minnesota. Lounge area adjacent to current periodicals. Special light fixtures create feeling of a high ceilinged area.

Missouri, Washington University. Current issues in alcove arrangement.

Maryland, Johns Hopkins University. Current journals next to elegant reading room.

Massachusetts, Amherst College. Low A-frame cases with issues held vertically.

Massachusetts, Harvard University, Countway Library. Current issues on top, back issues below. Issues held vertically tend to flap over.

Massachusetts, Harvard University, Radcliffe College. Spacious and handsome low cases.

Massachusetts, Harvard University. Radcliffe College. A corner arrangement with greater concentration than in island cases.

Indiana, Earlham College. Cases placed at forty-five degree angle to allow space for reading bench.

Indiana, Notre Dame University. Special double-faced cases designed to hold current issues facing reader, with back issues stored behind.

Indiana, Indiana University Research Library. For large collection flat shelving is used to conserve space.

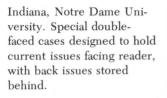

Iowa, University of Iowa. Typical current serials alcove in large university libraries.

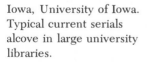

Ohio, Wooster College.
Note use of vertical dividers
to keep piles of journals in
order.

Oklahoma, University of
Oklahoma. A pleasant alcove
for reading current journals.

Oregon, Lewis and Clark
University. Current issues
and bound volumes in
separate room. Note dome
lighting — not good.

Oregon, Oregon State University. Specialized journals in alcoves.

Oregon, University of Oregon Science Library. Indexes shelved adjacent to current issues of journals.

Oregon, Portland State College. Social Science divisional journals. Similar arrangement in each of the divisional libraries.

Oregon, Southern Oregon College. Journals are kept in L-shaped alcove.

Pennsylvania, Beaver College. A small collection nicely housed. Various types of reading facilities nearby.

Pennsylvania, Bryn Mawr College. A pleasant lounge area for reading periodicals.

Pennsylvania, Drexel Institute. Special cases near staff technical processing and reference offices.

Pennsylvania, Kutztown State College. Microform readers kept behind the current issues cases.

Pennsylvania, Lafayette College. Indexes on tables near current journals.

Pennsylvania, Lehigh University, Science Library. A compact arrangement.

Pennsylvania, University of Pennsylvania Wharton School. A business school collection kept in low cases near entrance to library.

Rhode Island, Brown University. Current issues with faces showing, back issues behind the slanting shelves.

Scotland, Glasgow University. Current issues with faces showing, back issues behind.

South Dakota, University of South Dakota. Low window cases used for a variety of purposes. General periodicals in this area.

Sweden, Chalmers University. An attractive arrangement. Great chairs!

Tennessee, Belmont College. A small collection in a college library.

Tennessee, Fisk University. Lounge furniture near current issues.

Texas, Abilene Christian College. Small college library current serials display shelves.

Texas, Southern Methodist University, Science Library. Comfortable reading facilities near journal alcoves.

Utah, University of Utah. General periodicals kept in special lounge area, separate from specialized periodicals.

Washington, Pacific Lutheran University. Non-current issues of last volume kept in notebook binders below current issues. Good but expensive method.

Washington, Pacific Lutheran University. Pleasant periodical reading room, with serials librarians and records nearby.

Washington, D.C., Georgetown University Large area with lounge furniture nearby.

NEWSPAPERS

California, Chabot College. Special rack with hinged plastic cover for each paper. Keeps papers neat.

California, Chabot College. Others are spread out on sloping shelves.

Florida, University of Florida. Plastic hinged covers keep papers neat. Easy to use.

Georgia, Emory University.
Papers on poles in racks.

Indiana, Indiana University
Research Library. Papers
held in place by plastic
cover. An excellent system.

Minnesota, University
of Minnesota. Papers
shelved flat — one fold.

Texas, Rice University. New
kind of suspended bag.

Washington, Pacific Luth-
eran University. Papers
rolled and put in bin.

Wisconsin, University
of Wisconsin at Milwaukee.
Plastic covers hinged at top.

6. Technical Processes Departments

Housing a technical processes department is largely a matter of subdividing a large, open area by means of catalog cabinets, shelving, carrels, and room partitions. There are so many ways of organizing a technical processes division that no attempt will be made here to portray the various methods.

Architectural Intent

1. To provide open space that can be subdivided and rearranged freely. Organization changes continuously.

2. To provide higher light levels (up to 100 footcandles) than in the reading rooms.

3. To hold the noise of machinery and concentrations of people at acceptable sound levels.

4. Provisions for power and telephone wire outlets in almost all areas of the technical processes division. Computer consoles will also be needed.

5. To place offices and carrels so staff will have a sense of privacy yet not be isolated from essential working tools.

Cataloger's Carrels

Delaware, University of Delaware. Typical arrangement calls for book truck on right (or left) side with desk surface plus shelf for reference books; typewriter on opposite side.

England, East Anglia University. Staff has less visual privacy than is customary in the United States.

Florida, University of Florida. Visual dividers used. Bookcases in place of trucks. No shelf for reference books. Note pile of reference books on table.

France, University of Lyon. No visual privacy.

Georgia, Georgia Institute of Technology. Provides larger bookcase for reference books than is usual.

Germany, University of Frankfurt. Each cataloger has generous sized alcove.

Germany, University of Frankfurt. Cataloger handling microforms. Note two book trucks in alcove.

Illinois, University of Chicago. Cataloger's carrel. One of the earliest of this type. Has glass partition above dividers.

Illinois, Illinois State University, Normal. Four-place alcoves are in use.

Indiana, Indiana University. Administrative carrel for head of division.

Indiana, Indiana University. Carrel with microreader.

Indiana, Indiana University. Desk facing bookshelf forming divider between two alcoves. Book truck on aisle helps with privacy problem.

Massachusetts, Amherst College. Alcoves have generous shelf space behind each desk.

Massachusetts, Amherst College. Carrels along outer wall. Very good.

Michigan, Central Michigan University. An excellent carrel for catalogers.

Michigan, Grand Valley State College. Desks using wall shelves for reference books. Book trucks would be placed on aisle side.

Minnesota, University of Minnesota. Each carrel in group gives privacy on four sides. Has large number of carrels.

Minnesota, University of Minnesota. Office for head of technical processes. Glass walls for supervision.

North Carolina, Duke University. Small sized carrel.

North Carolina, Duke University. Large carrel.

North Carolina, University of North Carolina, Undergraduate Library. Bookcase forms visual barrier along aisle side.

Pennsylvania, Bryn Mawr College. Tall shelf divider between carrels.

Pennsylvania, Lafayette College. Carrels using wall shelves for reference books.

Scotland, Glasgow University. Generous work space and privacy on three sides.

Washington, Washington State University. Each person has separate room. More generous than is found in most libraries.

Washington, D.C., Georgetown University. Each cataloger has a desk next to shelves. Books kept on trucks.

AUTOMATION

California, University of California at San Diego. Cataloging information on microfiche.

Oregon, Oregon State University. On-line computer console for use of cataloging department.

SPECIAL FACILITIES

Colorado, University of Colorado. Cataloger's camera. Basic Xerox equipment with custom designed cradle to hold printed catalogs from which entries are photographed.

Indiana, Indiana University.
Cataloger's camera. Custom
design.

Iowa, University of Northern
Iowa. Sinks, cupboards and
work bench adjacent to technical processes staff.

7. Circulation Services

Architectural Intent

1. To place desk where it is clearly visible near entrance and so that line of traffic from desk to exit control is direct and does not cross traffic lines of people entering the building. In small buildings, usually to accommodate the reserve book and exit control functions.

2. To provide plenty of work space behind the desk to house the activities in either manual or computerized systems. To provide space for discharged books waiting to be reshelved.

3. To provide a clearly visible office for the head of public services, who has frequent consultations with the public.

4. To isolate circulation desk noises from the adjacent reading rooms.

Arizona, Arizona State University. A computerized system. Student is using printout list of books charged out.

California, University of California at Berkeley. Call board above desk to give readers status of books charged out.

California, University of California at Los Angeles, Research Library. Desk probably not large enough to handle traffic. Lounge chairs for those who have to wait.

California, Stanford University, Undergraduate Library. Note call board above desk. Borrower's number appears when his book has arrived. Note storage for earphones as well as shelves for books on reserve.

Canada, University of
Guelph. Books charged out
on computer at exit control.
Student combines both kinds
of work.

Florida, Florida Southern
College. Combines general
circulation, book return,
reserve book and exit control.
Note wooden baffles under
fluorescent lights.

Florida, University of Florida. A curved desk in front of
large work area. Entrance to
library is to right of desk.

Florida, University of
Tampa. Combination of general circulation and reserves.
Exit control desk at end of
desk.

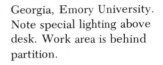

Georgia, Emory University.
Note special lighting above
desk. Work area is behind
partition.

Germany, University of
Frankfurt. Uses pneumatic
tubes for notifying pages.
Books returned by conveyor.

Idaho, University of Idaho.
Photo taken from back of
desk. This is a manual system.
Returned books are placed
directly on book shelves.

Idaho, University of Idaho.
Circulation lobby with exit
control at end of circulation
desk.

Indiana, Indiana University, Undergraduate Library. Combined general and reserve desks.

Indiana, Indiana University, Graduate Library. Indiana's custom designed patron's signal system. A book placed in a box flashes the box's number on call board above the boxes.

Indiana, Indiana University, Graduate Library. Call board system showing boxes and signals.

Iowa, University of Northern Iowa. Office for circulation librarian behind desk. Charging machine on left side of photograph.

Louisiana, Tulane University. A computerized circulation system behind desk.

Massachusetts, Amherst College. A properly designed layout. Books can be charged out at regular desk, or at exit control desk when no one is on duty at desk.

Michigan, Central Michigan University. General circulation at one end and reserves at the other.

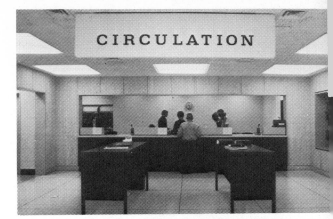

Minnesota, University
of Minnesota. Even with
manual system, desk is not
large.

Missouri, Washington Uni-
versity. An automated system. Students make heavy use
the print-out list of books
in use. Thus, an automated
system probably needs a larger desk than a manual system
although the charging appara-
tus requires less space.

Missouri, Washington Uni-
versity. Computerized charging system. Machine enclosed
to minimize noise. There
should be a sound barrier between desk and reading room.

New York, Wells College.
Combined reserve and general
circulation. Compare with
Radcliffe for size. Note card
catalogs attached to floor.

North Carolina, Duke University. Desk is to left of records alcove. Use of down lights above records is mistake. Lighting is uneven.

North Carolina, Duke University. The Duke desk from front. Handsome arrangement. Lighting bad over desk.

Oregon, Lewis and Clark University. A traditional manual desk arrangement from rear. Entrance to library is on left.

Oregon, University of Oregon, Science Library. Roller chute for book return system. Easy to work with and does not damage books.

Oregon, Portland State College. Good relationship between desk, card catalog, information desk at right. Photograph was taken from entrance.

Oregon, Portland State College. Circulation office behind desk. Efficient layout.

Oregon, Southern Oregon College. Simple system with work area behind partition.

Pennsylvania, Lafayette College. Combined general and reserve circulation system with exit control at far end of desk.

Pennsylvania, Lehigh University, Science Library. A computerized system — two machines, side by side.

Scotland, Glasgow University. Located in area where expansion would be difficult; but when the permanent entrance is installed, desk will be moved. A nearby "undergrad" library absorbs the heavy circulation use of its library system.

South Carolina, Clemson University. Here computer machinery is installed in circulation desk.

Tennessee, Fiske University. Combined system with checkout at general desk or at checkout desk when work load is heavy.

Texas, Southwestern University. Small system with good supervision for lobby and exit control. Library entrance, left.

Utah, University of Utah. Desks containing circulation records can be wheeled into work room behind as needed. Circulation desk is on left.

Washington, D.C., Georgetown University. Large area behind circulation desk. Book trucks stored on right. Computers in desk. Entrance at far end of room.

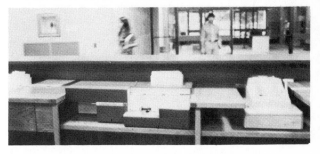

Washington, D.C., Georgetown University. Hardware for computerized system. Cash register for fines.

Wisconsin, Beloit College. A simple, combined system for small college. Entrance is on left.

Wisconsin, University of Wisconsin at Madison, Agriculture Library. Front of charging desk.

8. Reserve Book Services — Open and Closed

Because few academic libraries have enough copies of books heavily used as required reading in courses, these books are placed on a restricted circulation basis in one of two systems — direct access or closed access.

Architectural Intent

1. To place the reserve book desk as near the entrance as possible so that its heavy use will not disturb the rest of the library.

2. To combine the reserve and general circulation charging desk, whenever possible, to minimize administrative cost.

3. To provide students with a quick access catalog to the books on reserve.

Arizona, Arizona State University. Typical closed access reserve layout.

California, University of California at Berkeley, Undergraduate Library. A catalog of the books on reserve, arranged by department and by course.

Georgia, University of Georgia, Science Library. Closed access. Office for librarian accommodates negotiations between reserve librarian and faculty.

Illinois, University of Chicago. Cards arranged by department and course, as at University of California, Berkeley.

Illinois, University of Illinois, Undergraduate Library. Students get their own books (turnstile control), charge them out at desk, and read where they want to in library. Example of open access system.

Iowa, University of Iowa. An open access system. Students get their own books but charge them out before going into reading room.

Iowa, University of Northern Iowa. All reserves on closed access.

Massachusetts, Harvard University, Radcliffe College. Closed access in front. Open access at rear. Staff members are taking inventory.

Michigan, Eastern Michigan University. A closed reserve system with tables and carrels nearby for readers.

Minnesota, University of Minnesota. The closed reserve section of the reserve library. Many books are also on open access reserve.

Minnesota, University of Minnesota. Another example of reserve room catalog arranged by courses.

Minnesota, University of Minnesota. Open shelf collection to right. Desk for closed reserve to left.

Missouri, Washington University. An open access reserve system. Windows on right open on central atrium.

Oregon, Oregon Southern College. A closed reserve system.

Pennsylvania, University of Pennsylvania, Wharton School. Open access to books behind counter. Students enter at one gate and leave by another, where they charge out their books.

Scotland, Glasgow University. A closed reserve system.

Texas, University of Texas,
Undergraduate Library.
A closed access system.

Utah, University of Utah.
A closed access system.

9. The Catalog — In Card or Printed Form

Architectural Intent

1. To locate catalog near entrance.

2. To provide tables between rows of cabinets, or between cabinets, so that readers can examine the drawers without being in the way of other users.

3. To provide space for various forms of the catalog — in card drawers, in printed volumes, and eventually via computer consoles.

4. To place the catalog where it can expand adequately, where it can be easily consulted by the reference and technical processes staffs, and where its use noise will not be a source of annoyance to readers.

5. To provide high light levels — possibly 100 footcandles.

California, California Institute of Technology. In a small library this catalog takes little room and can be combined with the reference collection — as it is here in a divisional library.

California, University of California at San Diego. Automation. Computerized printout of the serials catalog.

California, University of California at Santa Cruz. Catalog in printed form. When kept open it takes as much room as a card catalog — assuming one needs more than one copy to distribute its users adequately. This is now being printed via Zerox 7000 and photo-offset methods.

California, University of California at Santa Cruz. Copies of the printed catalog on other floors — where volume of use does not require multiple copies — kept open.

Canada, University of Waterloo. Catalog placed along edges of room. Less convenient than when arranged in rows.

Delaware, University of Delaware. Alternate rows of cabinets and stand-up inspection tables — usually six feet between cabinet faces.

England, East Anglia University. Ledge in front of catalog causes traffic jams. Note also, reader sits down to use catalog.

Florida, University of Tampa. Catalog placed next to reference shelves. Reference desks behind. A good arrangement.

France, University of Aix-en-Provence, Droit Library. Most continental university libraries use low cabinets with tops for card inspection.

Georgia, Emory University. Cabinets higher than is customary. This is justified since readers use the stand-up table for searching the drawers.

Germany, Frankfurt University. Another example of European practice — low cabinets. Searchers work at the cabinets.

Germany, Giessen University. Another example of low cabinets in Europe.

Germany, Stuttgart University. Closer to American height with stand-up cabinets. This library has adapted more American practices than most European libraries.

Illinois, University of Chicago. A large university library catalog. Long rows with stand-up tables.

Illinois, Northwestern University. Study alcove at end of bank of cabinets. A good idea for readers who are making an extended search of a drawer.

Illinois, Northwestern University. A large university catalog arranged in typical manner.

Iowa, University of Northern Iowa. Placed in front lobby. Polaroid lens in light fixtures.

Maryland, Johns Hopkins University. In lobby with reference books behind. Note drop lights — give poor lighting over catalog.

Massachusetts, Boston University. Telephone jacks in cabinets enable staff to plug in and talk with other staff. Particularly useful when technical processes staff is housed at a distance. Note tall cabinets. Same as Emory University.

Massachusetts, Harvard University, Countway Library. Close to printed national catalogs, which are used to locate books not in Countway.

Massachusetts, Harvard University, Radcliffe College. Catalog is placed near reference collection and reference librarian. Note vertical file (pamphlets) behind counter. Note custom designed light fixtures.

Michigan, Central Michigan University. A standard layout. Light fixtures are coordinated with cabinets.

Michigan, Eastern Michigan University. Uses top for inspection surface. Notice how this causes crowding.

Michigan, Wayne University Medical Library. Note telephone at end of cabinets for staff use.

Minnesota, University of Minnesota. Large catalog with catalog information desk in front. A good layout.

Missouri, Washington University. A standard layout. Well planned.

New Zealand, University of
Auckland. Public catalog near
reference area. Follows European idea of low cabinets. A
louverall type of lighting.

North Carolina, Duke Uni-
versity. Double inspection
shelf between cabinets. Also
tables between ranges.

North Carolina, Elon Col-
lege. Small college catalog.
L-shaped.

Ohio, John Carroll Uni-
versity. Note glass
partition between catalog
and reference department
in rear.

Ohio, Ohio Northern University. Careful attention to details. Attractive and convenient.

Oklahoma, University of Oklahoma. Note inspection table built around large column.

Oregon, Pacific Lutheran University. Reading lists at end of catalog.

Pennsylvania, Lafayette College. A typical layout.

Pennsylvania, University
of Pennsylvania. A large university catalog. Chairs are for
use of staff filing cards or
revising the catalog.

Pennsylvania, Temple Uni-
versity. Card catalog between
entrance and circulation desk.
Plenty of room for expansion.
Low cabinets using tops for
searching. Note psychedelic
ceiling lighting.

Rhode Island, Brown Uni-
versity. Reference collection
behind card catalog. A satisfactory layout.

Rhode Island, Brown Uni-
versity. Telephone jacks in
cabinets.

Scotland, Glasgow University. Follows practice of inserting sheets in binders.

South Carolina, Clemson University. Looking at catalog from circulation desk office and reference collection behind catalog.

South Dakota, University of South Dakota. Catalog is adjacent to reference collection and near entrance. Microfilm readers and photocopy machines are available. Note light fixtures at right angles to cabinets for flexibility.

Utah, University of Utah. Librarian uses telephone to communicate with someone elsewhere in building.

10. Photocopy Services

Architectural Intent

To provide three types of facilities for making photocopies of library materials: 1) To place self-service photocopy machines throughout the library where readers can make their own copies; 2) to place machines near the circulation desk and the serials department office for staff use; and 3) to provide a complete photography laboratory including microfilming and photostat machines. Sometimes this laboratory provides complete graphics services.

Georgia, Georgia Institute of Technology. The machines have been placed in passageway linking old building and addition.

Minnesota, University of Minnesota. A copying service near the central circulation desk. Counter placed at end of a narrow corridor obviously causes crowding.

North Carolina, Duke University. Behind the scenes of a complete photo laboratory.

Oregon, Lewis and Clark University. Photocopier on main floor near reference desk. A self-service machine.

Pennsylvania, Lehigh University, Science Library. A small photocopying room next to circulation desk.

11. Administrative Offices

Although there is no reason in a large university library why the central administrative offices need to be on the main floor, library directors like to be where the action is, and where they can be reached quickly by visitors. Hence, the administrative suite is frequently placed on the main floor. In the small college libraries, however, the librarian usually works closely with all the acquisition staff; therefore the administrative office is usually located as close as possible to the main floor center of activity.

The symbolism involved with the director's office is something he may or may not be willing to discuss openly. Perhaps the architect should consult the director's secretary or wife to find out what he really has in mind.

Architectural Intent

1. Small, modest versus large, impressively equipped office.

2. The presence of a conference table in the main office, and the nature of the work space for the librarian.

3. The need for a conference or seminar room adjacent to the central office for meetings of committees or heads of departments.

4. Where to place offices for associate and assistant directors. Are they to be in the central suite or in the respective work areas for public services and technical processes?

5. Presence of blackboard and tack boards for discussions of budgets, organization charts, and building plans.

6. How to place the desks of the secretarial pool so that visitors will know which one to approach.

Arizona, Arizona State University. A simple formal office with work ledge behind desk and a half dozen chairs for visitors.

Delaware, University of Delaware. Small modest office with desk facing away from entrance. Rather unusual.

Georgia, Georgia Institute of Technology. A special room for the library board or trustees.

Iowa, University of Iowa. Staff conference room near director's office.

Louisiana, Tulane University. Director's office and desk beyond secretary's desk. Offices for associates on opposite side of room.

Maryland, Johns Hopkins
University. Director's office
beyond secretary's desk.
Lounge chairs for visitors.

Massachusetts, Harvard University, Countway Medical
Library. Small office with
conversation table in foreground.

Michigan, Central Michigan
University. Fairly large office
with work shelf and storage
cupboard behind director's
desk. A four-place conference
table in foreground.

Minnesota, University of Minnesota. Office of the librarian (often called associate director). Work shelf at end of room. In large universities there is usually a suite of offices for associates and assistants with central secretarial pool.

Pennsylvania, Lehigh University, Science Library. Small office with desk, work table, and chair for visitors.

Scotland, Edinburgh University. Librarian uses a low conversation table in corner of office.

Tennessee, Scarritt College.
This librarian obviously
works with books more than
is customary in large libraries.

Tennessee, Vanderbilt University. Most university directors have a staff organization
chart, campus plan, or budget
display behind the desk.

Tennessee, Vanderbilt University. A staff conference
room adjacent to director's
office.

Washington, D.C., George-
town University. Large office
for director with conference
table at rear and cupboard on
left side.

12. Directories

It is difficult, even in the best arranged libraries, to find one's way around. To offset this difficulty, librarians and architects attempt to design directories to inform the reader where to find his materials. A few are pictured.

California, University of California at Berkeley, Undergraduate Library. The area at top is now used for classrooms. Other divisions of library are clearly marked.

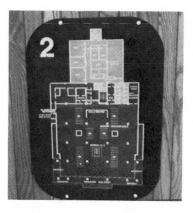

Canada, Guelph University. A specially designed cabinet provides floor layouts and other helpful information.

Canada, University of Waterloo. Another kind of directory — for reference materials.

Canada, University of Waterloo. Floor plan for each floor located on each stair landing.

England, York University.
Special case for directory for
each floor.

Illinois, Northwestern University. Floor plans of each
floor.

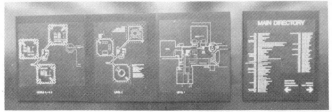

Michigan, Eastern Michigan
University. Directory on easel
near entrance.

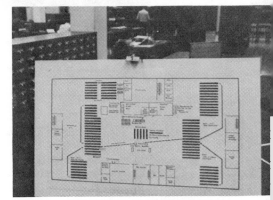

New York, State University
of New York at Albany. Good
directory for all four floors.

Washington, Pacific Lutheran University. Staff directory, including student assistants.

Washington, Pacific Lutheran University. Floor plans for each floor.

13. Floor Plans

a. *Fixed Core Service Elements.* There are several basic theories for locating these elements.

The *corner plan* (University of North Texas at Denton, Glasgow University):

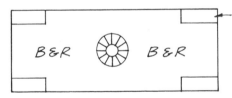

← Stairways, elevators, toilets, janitor closets

The *central spine* (Brigham Young, San Fernando State College, Arizona State University):

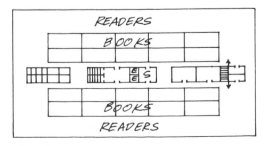

Typical floor above the first.

The *side plan* (Nebraska Home Economics, Wooster, Beloit, University of Northern Iowa, Nevada, Pacific Lutheran University):

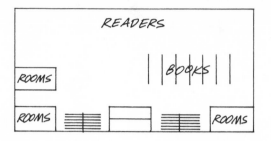

In this type of building the core units usually go up through the center of the above-ground structure.

The *end plan* (Emory, Cornell):

It cannot be proven that any one form for a library is better than the others because much depends on one's philosophy of organization. The corner plan places the greatest concentration of readers in the center of the building but the central spine plan, in practice, moves people well and permits the development of interesting reading centers along the outer walls. (University of Northern Iowa, Clark University)

b. *Examples of Main Floor Layouts.*

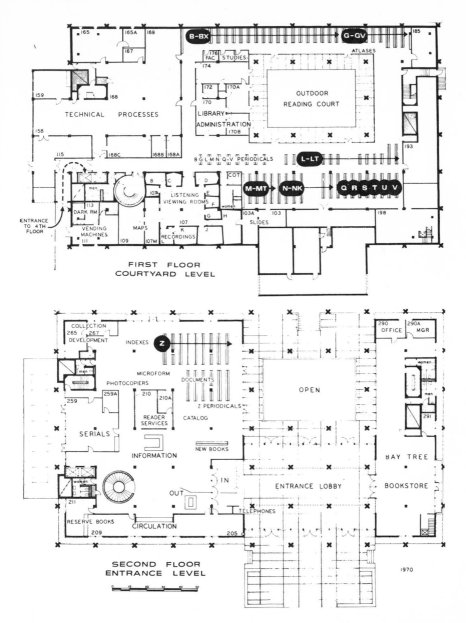

California, University of California at Santa Cruz. Entrance lobby and courtyard divide building into two parts — bookstore on right, library on left. Library keys are clearly visible with all main floor elements in their right place. Technical processes department and administration offices are on floor above. Core elements at one end. Excellent plan.

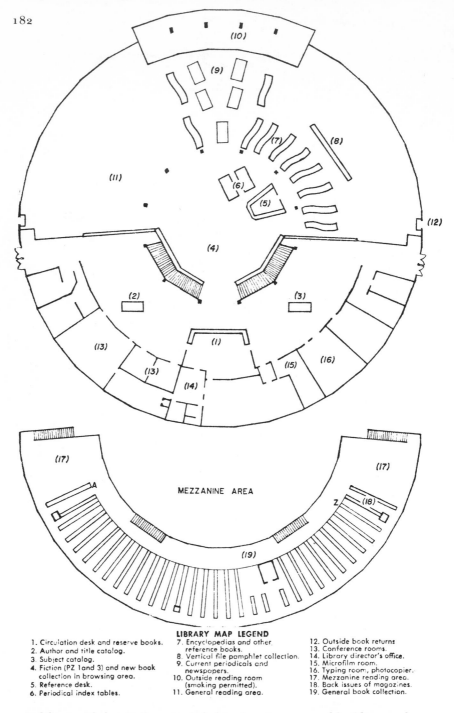

LIBRARY MAP LEGEND

1. Circulation desk and reserve books.
2. Author and title catalog.
3. Subject catalog.
4. Fiction (PZ 1 and 3) and new book collection in browsing area.
5. Reference desk.
6. Periodical index tables.
7. Encyclopedias and other reference books.
8. Vertical file pamphlet collection.
9. Current periodicals and newspapers.
10. Outside reading room (smoking permitted).
11. General reading area.
12. Outside book returns.
13. Conference rooms.
14. Library director's office.
15. Microfilm room.
16. Typing room, photocopier.
17. Mezzanine reading area.
18. Back issues of magazines.
19. General book collection.

California, Chabot College. Included to show how a round building can be arranged. In a community college, where book collection does not have to be expanded, round shape is satisfactory.

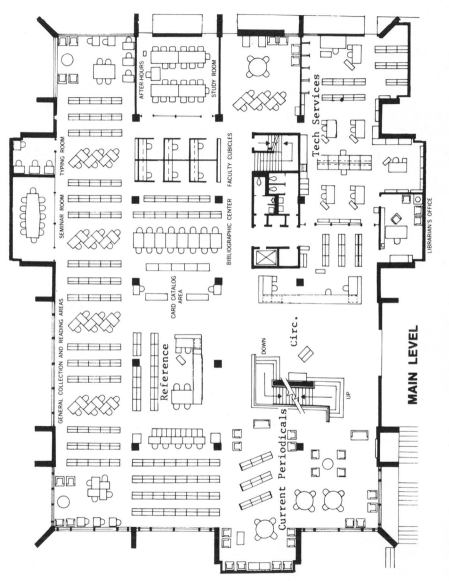

California, Westmont College. A pleasant small college plan. Main stairway is centered in open atrium.

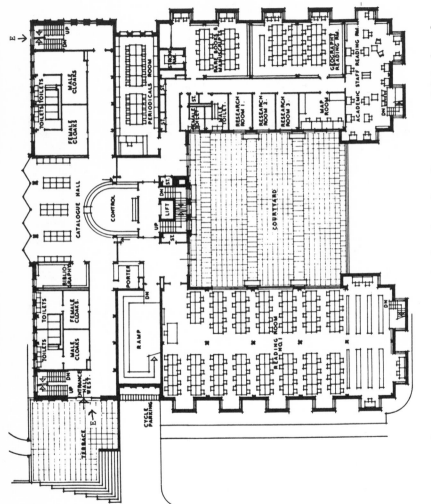

England, Exeter University. Access to bookstacks and reading rooms on left is cleared by porter, with ramp to first floor elevator and central stairway. Patrons must walk through tables of readers to reach books at end of room. Specialized collections are in opposite wing. Current periodicals are in room adjacent to central desk.

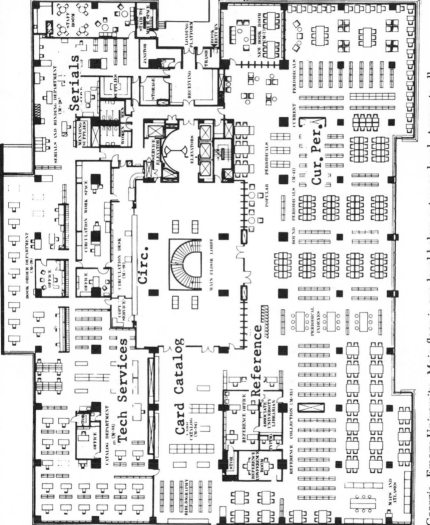

Georgia, Emory University. Main floor is one level below entrance level. Access to all parts of this level open to all. Entrance to bookstack in tower is controlled by I.D. card mechanism in front of elevators. A well thought-out plan in terms of assumptions governing it.

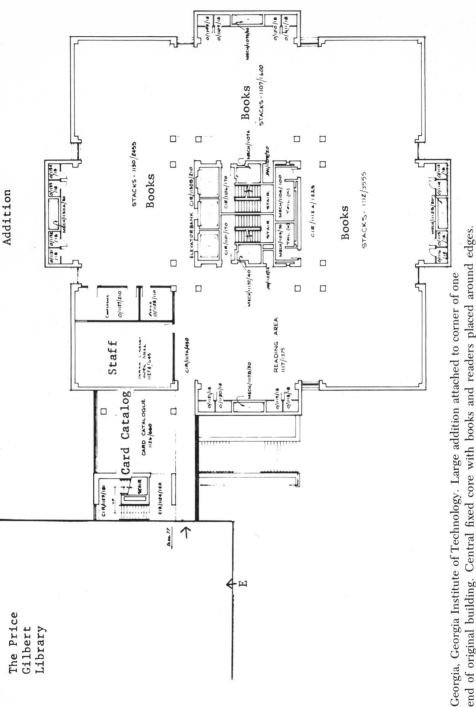

Georgia, Georgia Institute of Technology. Large addition attached to corner of one end of original building. Central fixed core with books and readers placed around edges.

Illinois, University of Chicago. A beautifully planned main floor. Note that gate at "X" to left of entrance can be closed and reserve library operated as all night study room. Each element is in right place. This level open to all. Entrance to other levels controlled at "A." Separate entrance to library school wing.

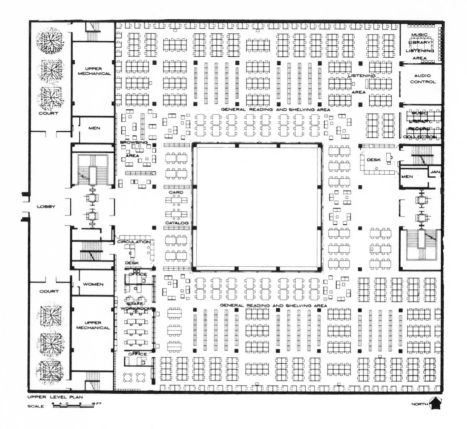

Illinois, University of Illinois, Undergraduate Library. Underground library with large central courtyard. Books and readers are grouped in blocks. Entrance from street level at left with card catalog straight ahead. Audio-visual area in rear.

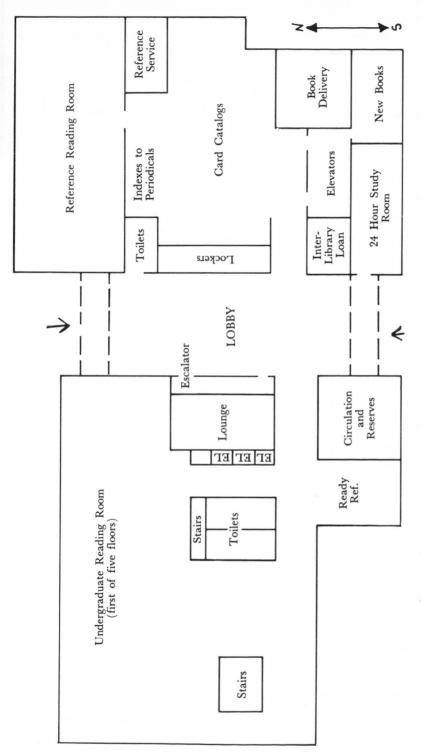

Indiana, Indiana University, general and undergraduate libraries. Undergraduate collections are on left side, central lobby, with general or research library, on right. Note large locker room off lobby. Lower level of undergraduate collection includes cafeteria. Research collections are in upper stories with entrance control point in elevator area. A beautifully planned layout.

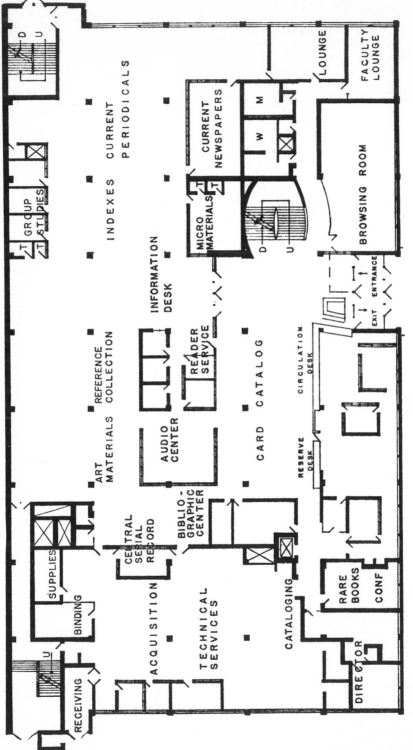

Iowa, University of Northern Iowa. One of the few nearly perfect library main floor plans. Every element in exactly the right place. Building is now being expanded at rear.

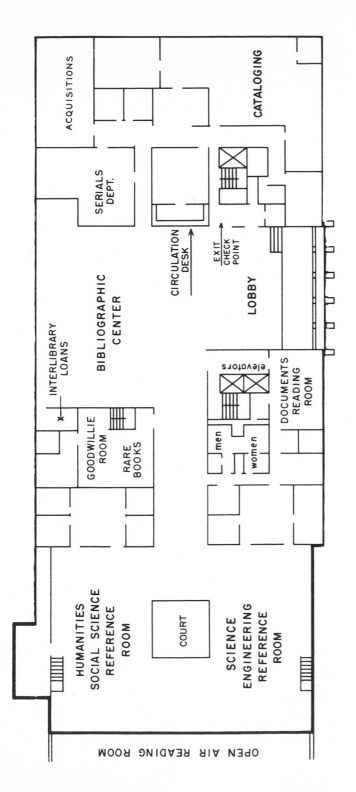

Maryland, Johns Hopkins University, Central Library. Large university library with top level entrance. From Charles Street entrance one descends one level to main floor. Main card catalog and reference collection are just beyond lobby. Divisional reference centers are dispersed through building. A small rare books room is on this floor, with rare book collections on level below.

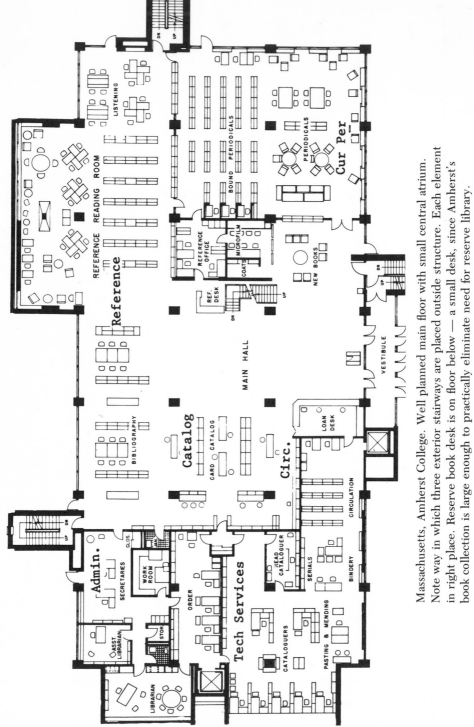

Massachusetts, Amherst College. Well planned main floor with small central atrium. Note way in which three exterior stairways are placed outside structure. Each element in right place. Reserve book desk is on floor below — a small desk, since Amherst's book collection is large enough to practically eliminate need for reserve library.

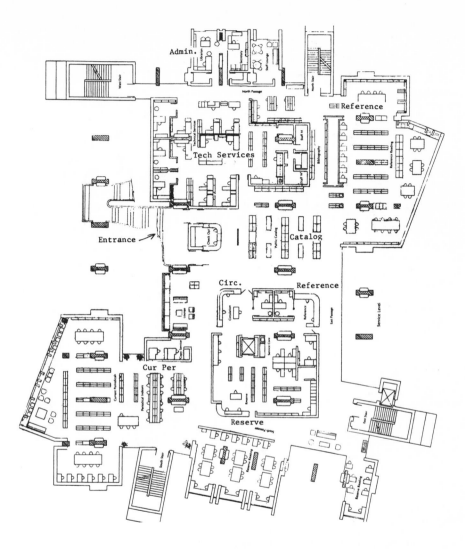

Massachusetts, Clark University. Conventional main floor layout with
interesting central core with three desks (circulation, reference, and reserve)
and central work area. Many varied-shaped reading areas on outer edges
of building.

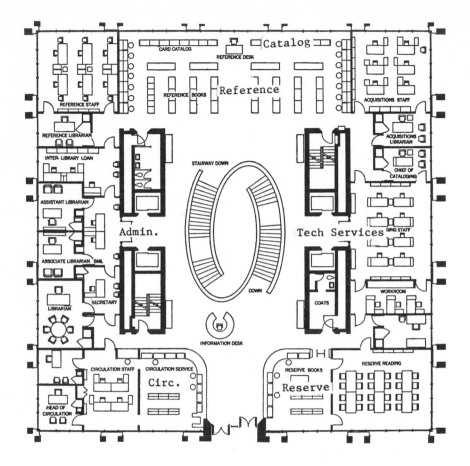

Massachusetts, Harvard University, Countway Medical Library. Large medical science library with large central atrium. Interesting feature: one can see down main stairway to current periodicals below reference desk.

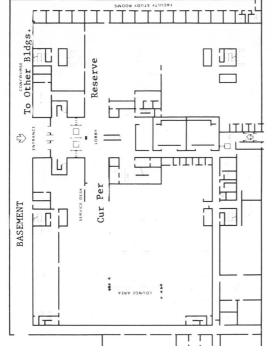

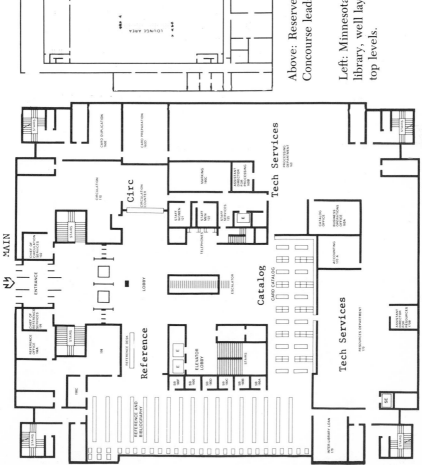

Above: Reserves and current periodicals on basement level. Concourse leads to other buildings underground.

Left: Minnesota, University of Minnesota. Large research library, well layed out. Administration and rare books on top levels.

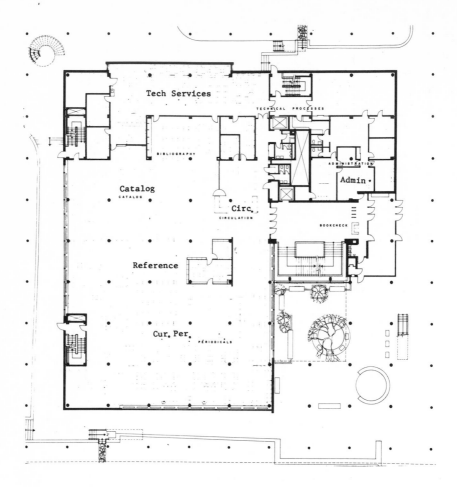

Missouri, Washington University. Still regarded as one of best planned
university libraries in United States. Two weaknesses in main floor layout:
circulation desk noise penetrates reference readers, and technical processes
area is too small. All elements, however, are in good relationship. Note
placing of atrium where it does not interfere with traffic patterns.

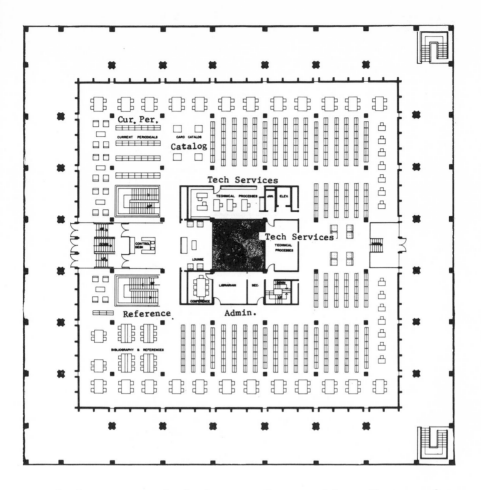

Nebraska, University of Nebraska, Home Economics Library. Entrance and control point on left. Card catalog, reference, and current periodicals at rear and front. Central core contains atrium in center with offices, work rooms, seminars, administration, etc. opening off atrium. Books and seating around outer edges of building.

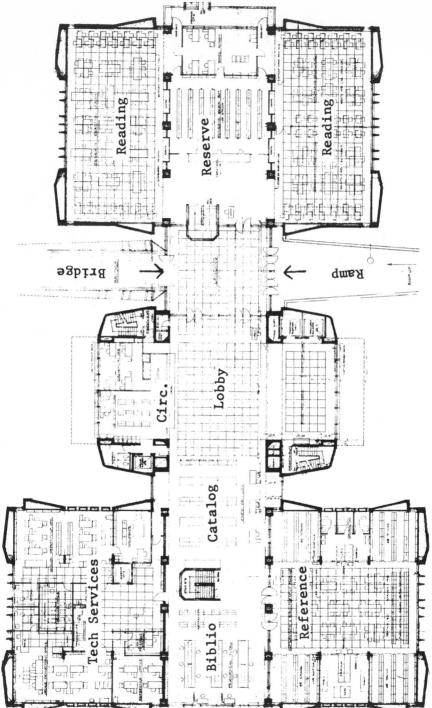

New York, Hofstra University. Large platform with tall tower. Hofstra's character as a
commuting university whose students are habitually in a hurry explains large reserve
library on main level. Entrance to tower is by stairways and elevator off lobby.

2nd Floor

New York, Wells College. Library placed on side hill site. Entrance at top (via bridge) and bottom. Many shapes and levels with many different kinds of reading facilities give building its monumental character. Main floor elements rather crowded into upper end of this floor.

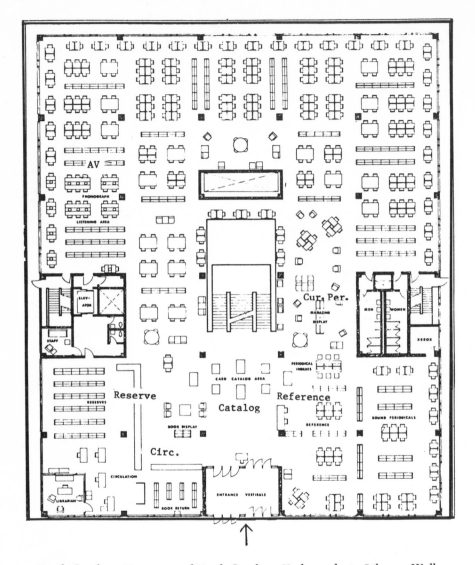

North Carolina, University of North Carolina, Undergraduate Library. Well arranged main floor. Reference department and periodicals collection are smaller in an undergraduate library than are required in a research library. Keys are placed directly in front of entrance. Notice how planners have infused bookshelves and reader stations.

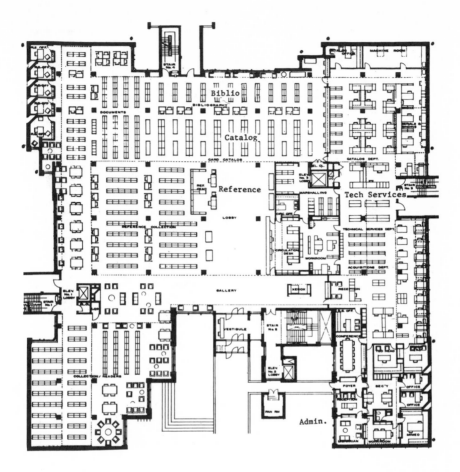

Ohio, Oberlin College (under construction). Oberlin has a large collection —
the equal of many universities — particularly in its reference department.
This main floor layout is convenient for users, except for hidden location
of reference staff, which may turn out to be problem.

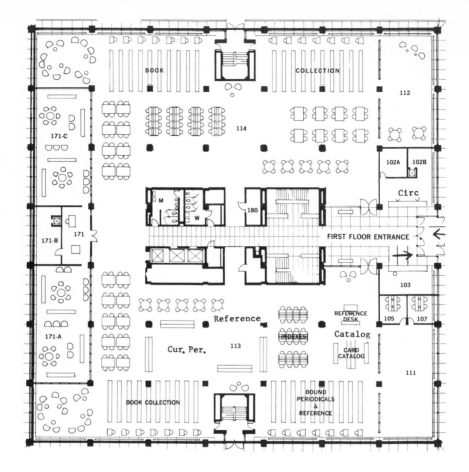

Pennsylvania, Pittsburgh University. Fixed core elements in center. Reference center on left side. There are no rooms for reference staff on this level.
Browsing and smoking rooms across rear. Floor is large enough to house two groups of book collection. Large atriums on either side of central core.

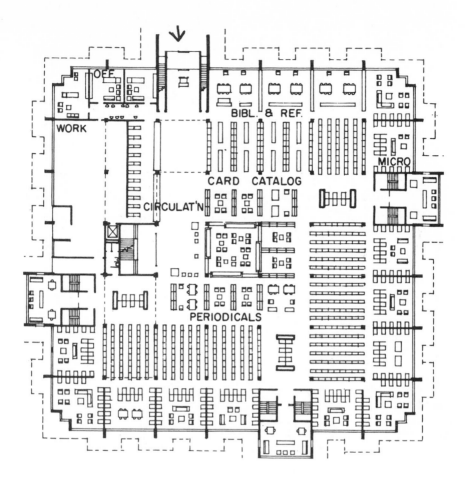

Rhode Island, Providence College. Small college library. Compact and convenient.

Texas, Abilene Christian College. Attractive and well arranged library.
Combined reference shelving and carrels are unusual and nice. Use of color
in building is outstanding, as are its provisions for audiovisual materials.
One of best college library buildings in United States.

Washington, D.C., Georgetown University. Another well planned layout for an urban university.

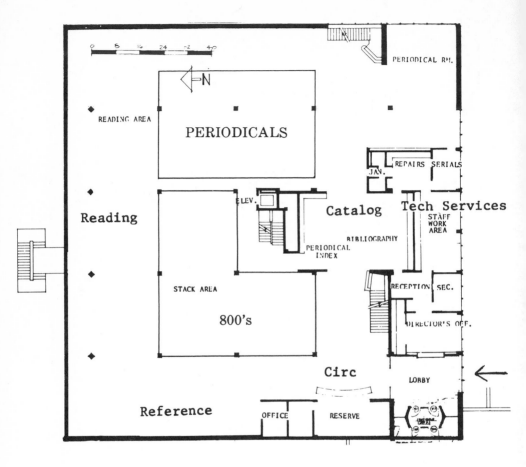

Wisconsin, Beloit College. A book-centered main floor: the President wanted
it that way. View from lobby through bookstacks to handsome lounge area
across rear of library is fine. Card catalog area a bit tight, as is technical
processes area. An attractive library.

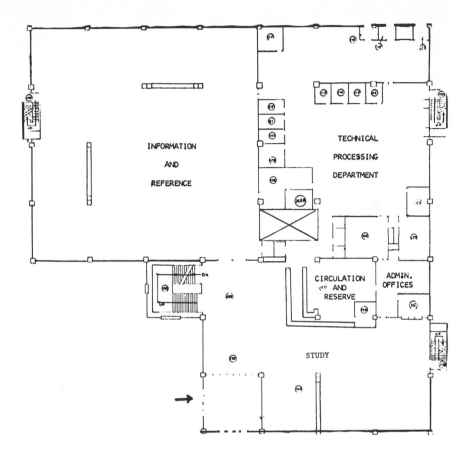

Wisconsin, University of Wisconsin at Milwaukee. Well planned layout. Large study area serves as lobby and absorbs sound in heavily used urban university library.

A Student at Ease Among the Books

V

Books and Readers—
People and Books

A.   BASIC SYSTEMS

IN the old fixed-function building the problem of how to mix facilities for readers and books was not a major one because books went into the multi-tier stacks (with carrels for graduate students around the perimeters), readers into separate reading rooms, faculty into small studies, and graduate classes into seminars.

In the modular buildings any one of the above functions can be placed anywhere in the open spaces. This permits the librarian to develop whatever mix his philosophy of organization suggests. This freedom is essential in a contemporary academic library, for the reasons stated in Chapter II. But it forces the librarian and architect to work together in placing the facilities so that they not only function the way the librarian wants them to, but also so that the building is attractive and has environmental form and quality.

The following principles seem to have produced the results that architects, librarians and readers appreciate.

Arrange bookshelving and reader stations together in such a way that the following conditions hold:

1. Readers should be able to find books easily. This means that the blocks of bookstack ranges are placed so that readers can follow the classification sequences without encountering confusing interruptions and frequent changes of direction.

2. Readers should be able to find comfortable and appropriate furniture, i.e. tables, carrels of varying kinds and sizes, lounge chairs, discussion rooms, etc., close to the books and other media they are using.

To accomplish these results, architects have used the following techniques:

1. Placing the bookstack ranges between the entrance and the reader stations. This enables the reader to get his books on his way to the place where he studies.

2. Placing bookstack ranges in blocks with reader stations at the ends or between blocks rather than using alternate rows of ranges and reader facilities. The larger the book collections, the more it becomes necessary to formalize the arrangements. This contrasts with the old concept of forcing readers to walk through reading rooms to get at wall shelving around the rooms. Supervision of readers by librarians seems to be unnecessary.

3. Limiting the length of bookstack ranges to between twenty-one and thirty feet; providing visual guides to help the reader connect the end of a classification sequence in one block to its beginning in the next block; running all the ranges in one direction.

4. Arranging traffic patterns so that people moving through the stacks are not a source of visual or noise annoyance to readers.

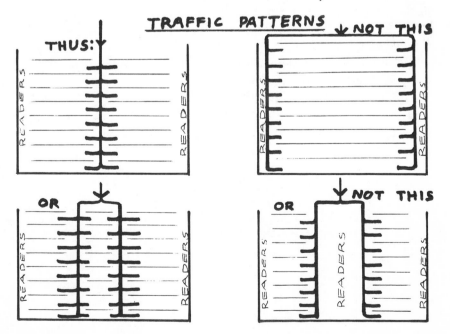

To avoid excessive dispersal of the bookstacks, it is not wise to run alternate rows of bookstacks and carrels. Instead, use blocks of ranges.

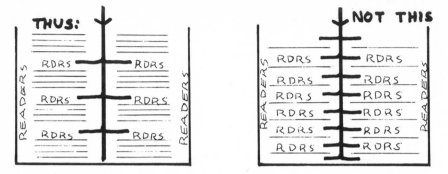

5. Placing various kinds of furniture in each reading area and doing this in such a manner that each type is placed in an appropriate environment. Thus, lounge chairs are clustered in a "living room" arrangement with a "framed view" window nearby; intensive study carrels have no visual distractions; rooms for discussions are available.

6. Fixed core elements are stacked so that readers find them in the same place on each floor level.

7. Philosophies of organization. The floor plan layouts and photographs in Chapter IV reflect the fact that there is no one way to relate books and people. There are many ways of achieving the results librarians have in mind.

The arrangement of facilities alone has not always produced the desired results. The quality of the lighting, carpeted floors, good furniture design and other environmental factors have been important.

B. Carrels — Reading Room and Tables

Arizona, Arizona State University. Two-place carrels. Shelf has no light overhead. Adjacent to bookstacks.

California, California Institute of Technology. Carrels placed next to windows with view of campus. Fixed shelf with no light fixture.

California, University of California at Berkeley, Undergraduate Library. Reading rooms full of carrels. See bookstack ranges in rear.

California, University
of California at Los Angeles,
Undergraduate Library. A
multi-tier bookstack con-
verted to undergraduate
reading room. Several types
of carrels four feet, six
inches long. Each carrel
uses two stack modules.

California, University
of California at Los Angeles,
Undergraduate Library. A
row of three-foot carrels in
stacks. Side openings.

California, University
of California at Los Angeles
Three-place carrels in reading room, with no shelves.

California, University of
of California at San Diego.
A reading alcove at end of
block of stacks.

California, University
of California at San Diego.
A row of carrels situated
between stack ranges.

California, University
of California at San Diego,
Medical Library. The cen-
tral stack block has carrels
on each of three sides. Each
is four feet long.

California, University
of California at San Diego.
Stand-up tables for using reference books. Sloping surfaces are less frequently
used, but seem appropriate.

California, Stanford University, Undergraduate Library.
Tables with low dividers.

California, Stanford University, Undergraduate Library. High dividers with coat hooks. Notice cupboard under work surface.

California, Westmont College. Carrels placed zigzag offer no particular advantage except variety.

Canada, Guelph University. A large block of carrels with lights under shelf. Research carrels on mezzanine in background.

Canada, University of Waterloo. Two-place carrel. Shelves with lights underneath. Note fenestration.

Colorado, University of Colorado. Four-foot carrels. No lights under shelves. Result: shadows.

Colorado, University of Colorado. Carrels with listening equipment attached.

England, Essex University. Nine-foot tables with divider. Notice light fixtures. These can be run in any direction.

England, Lancaster University. Carrels with bookcase at end of pair. Note lack of lighting in inner carrel.

England, Lancaster University. An excellent reading room carrel. In rows about twenty feet long. Similar idea is found in University of Chicago research carrels.

Finland. Helsinki Technical University. European University libraries usually provide tables with readers all facing in same direction. In this library both tables and chairs are more commodious than usual. Note ceiling lighting as opposed to individual table lamps.

Florida, University of Jacksonville. Tables in center, carrels around edge.

Georgia, Emory University. Eight places on a single table. Economical. Shelf but no lighting.

Germany, University of Frankfurt. German students are accustomed to tables in large reading rooms. No one ever bothers his neighbors in a German library!

Illinois, University of Chicago. Reading room and research carrels.

Illinois, University of Chicago. Tables, reading room carrels and research carrels.

Indiana, Earlham College. Placed on the diagonal along outer wall. A rather small working surface.

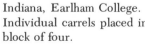

Indiana, Earlham College. Individual carrels placed in block of four.

Indiana, Notre Dame University. A four-place reading room carrel for a football player, obviously.

Indiana, Notre Dame University. A few sloping top tables provided for those who prefer them.

Idaho, University of Idaho. Small carrels in stack alcoves in sequence.

Iowa, Luther College. Four-place carrels in stack alcoves.

Louisiana, Tulane University. Rather large built-in carrels with locked boxes, adjacent to bookstacks.

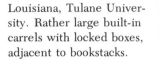

Massachusetts, Clark University. Bays with built-in carrels along outer wall of library.

Massachusetts, Tufts University. A wall of pods. A great place to put your feet on the table and lean back.

Michigan, the Herman Miller Educational Laboratory. Several examples of units adaptable to different types of facilities. This one houses a computer console.

Michigan, The Herman Miller Educational Laboratory. This type suitable for faculty research study.

Michigan, The Herman Miller Educational Laboratory. A writing table in a bookshelf.

Michigan, The Herman Miller Educational Laboratory. A four-place swastika carrel.

Minnesota, University
of Minnesota. Carrels in a
reserve book room.

Minnesota, University
of Minnesota. Research type
of carrel. Very poor lighting.

Missouri, Stephens College.
Two-place carrels that can
be closed and locked. They
are custom built.

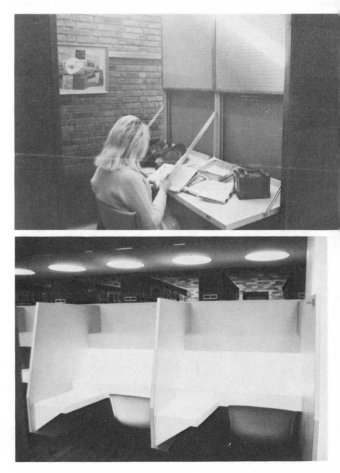

New Mexico, College of
Santa Fe. Generous table
surface space. Light under
shelf. Dropped shelf for
typing. Opening in back wall
for access to wiring.

New Mexico, College of Santa Fe. Ten-inch-wide spine separates the thirty-foot row of carrels and provides access to cables, wires, etc. Carrels attached to columns.

New York, State University of New York at Albany. Reading room carrels near lounge furniture.

North Carolina, Duke University. Carrels for researchers. These are assigned.

North Carolina, Elon College. Carrels in reading room — singles between tables and bookshelves.

North Carolina, University
of North Carolina, Under-
graduate Library. Several
types of carrels mixed in
with tables.

Ohio, Ohio Northern Uni-
versity. An interesting kind
of carrel at end of reading
room. Bays at opposite end
are furnished as faculty
studies. Outer wall is saw-
toothed in design.

Ohio, Wooster College.
Professor and students
confer in reading room carrel.

Oklahoma, Oklahoma Chris-
tian University. A large
room filled with carrels.

Oklahoma, Oklahoma Christian University. Each student has his own carrel. Contains dial access listening equipment. About four feet, six inches long.

Oregon, Portland State College. Carrels along outer walls.

Pennsylvania, Kutztown State College. Carrels facing wall. Saves space but students feet damage the wall. Some people do not like to face a wall.

Pennsylvania, Lehigh University, Science Library. Carrels along outer wall.

Pennsylvania, University
of Pennsylvania. Six-place
carrels in stack area. Note
bare fluorescent tubes.

Pennsylvania, Pittsburgh
University. Undergraduate
reading room under the
atrium. Bookshelves are
beyond carrels.

Rhode Island, Brown Uni-
versity. Two-place carrels
near reference shelves.

Scotland, Edinburgh University. Small tables and carrels near bookshelves.

Scotland, Glasgow University. Carrels with locked boxes in corner of room.

Tennessee, Scarritt College. Individual carrels along wall.

Tennessee, Vanderbilt University. Two-place carrels in stack alcove make a good arrangement.

Texas, Southwestern University. Carrels near books and faculty studies.

Texas, University of Texas, Undergraduate Library. Low carrel dividers. Adjacent to group study rooms.

Washington, Pacific Lutheran University. Large carrels near reference collection.

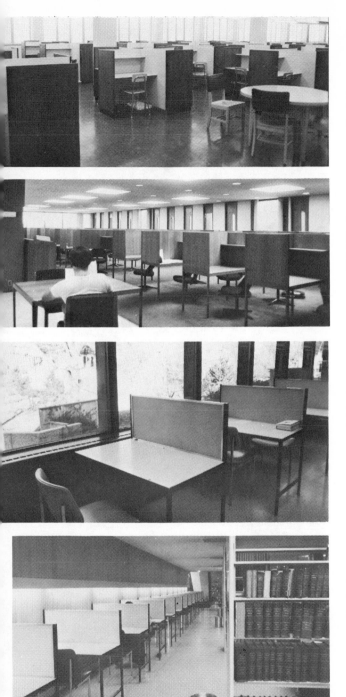

Washington, Washington State University. A large area filled with carrels. Offers privacy for a large student body.

Washington, D.C., Georgetown University. Carrels located along outer edge of bookstacks.

Wisconsin, Beloit College. Pleasant study carrels along wall with a view.

Wisconsin, Beloit College. Well lighted carrels along interior wall.

Wisconsin, University of
Washington at Madison,
Agriculture Library. Six-
place reading room carrels.

Wisconsin, University
of Wisconsin at Madison,
Agriculture Library. Tables
and carrels.

Wisconsin, University
of Wisconsin at Madison,
Agriculture Library. Tables
along edge of atrium.

C. CARRELS FOR RESEARCH

Traditionally, university libraries give graduate students an
assigned carrel or study where they can leave their books and
papers. To avoid the problem of under-utilization, some libraries
assign stack locker boxes to students and expect them to do their
reading at any carrel not in use.

Architectural Intent

1. To place the carrels near book collections but in areas where
privacy and quietness are to be found.

2. To provide a well lighted table space usually two-by-four feet or more, with some kind of locked cupboard for personal papers, books and objects.

Arizona, Arizona State University. A series of locked carrels along outside wall of reading rooms.

California, University of California at Los Angeles. Regular carrels near group of locked boxes.

California, University of California at Los Angeles. Carrels with lockers and lockable booktrucks. Plastic sides can be locked. Each truck is assigned to one student, who may take it anywhere in library.

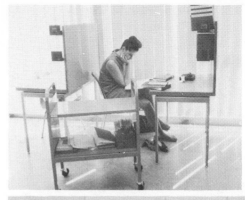

California, University
of California at Los Angeles.
Book truck — carrel in use.

California, Stanford University. Lockers below table
surface.

Canada, Guelph University.
A combined carrel and
locker case. Each case has
two lockers, one each side.

Florida, Florida Southern
College. Small rooms for
privacy.

Georgia, Emory University. Assigned carrels along stack walls.

Germany, University of Frankfurt. Research carrel, about five feet long.

Illinois, University of Chicago. Shows layout of carrels with lockers on back edge. One of best of its type in United States.

Illinois, University of Chicago. Each graduate student is assigned a locker and works at any nearby carrel. Locker doors hinge from bottom.

Indiana, Indiana University. Assigned carrels for graduate students in bookstacks.

Louisiana, Tulane University. Assigned lockers with unassigned carrels for graduate students. A row of these is placed between blocks of bookstacks.

Maryland, Johns Hopkins University. Row of graduate student carrels. All have lights below shelf and overhead. Lockers for each. All hang on stack columns.

Massachusetts, Clark University. Row of assigned carrels along outer wall next to bookstacks.

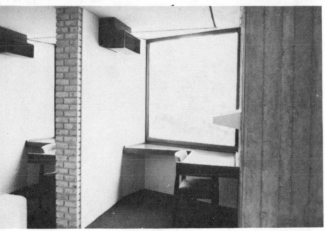

Massachusetts, Clark University. Built-in research carrel.

Michigan, Michigan Technological University. Research carrels built in.

Missouri, Washington University. Assigned carrels near faculty studies in background.

New York, Cornell University. Research carrels with lockers across aisle.

New York, Cornell University. Research carrels with steel mesh locked doors.

Ohio, Bowling Green University. A "garage" for carrel trucks. When student uses one he chooses an empty carrel and works there.

Ohio, Ohio Northern University. Built-in rooms at end of reading room. Walls placed at angle to give saw-tooth effect.

Oklahoma, University of Oklahoma. Carrels with cage-type walls. Not much visual privacy.

Oregon, University of Oregon, Science Library. Locked carrels. Front doors open to give privacy.

Oregon, University of Oregon, Science Library. Doors open show carrel in use.

Pennsylvania, Lafayette
College. Four carrels in
seminar room for special
students.

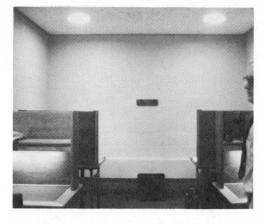

Pennsylvania, University
of Pennsylvania. Carrels at
end of ranges in bookstacks.

Rhode Island, Brown Uni-
versity. Carrels with shelves
above table and locker across
aisle.

Scotland, Edinburgh University. Research carrel with locker below.

Texas, Rice University. Two types of research carrels in bookstacks.

Washington, Pacific Lutheran University. Carrels equipped for dial access listening.

Washington, Pacific Lutheran University. Group of large three-place carrels in a room.

Lockers — With or Without Research Carrels

California, University
of California at San Diego.
Boxes are hung on stack
columns and can be added
as needed.

Canada, Guelph University.
Excellent arrangement for
research. Locker unit has
two compartments, one
facing front, the other the
rear. These carrels are not
assigned, but lockers are.

Georgia, Georgia Institute
of Technology. In the new
addition, groups of lockers are
placed near carrels.

Iowa, University of Northern Iowa. Group of lockers off reading room.

Michigan, Central Michigan University. Lockers are in front lobby.

Pennsylvania, Lehigh University. Lockers are in stack room.

South Carolina, Clemson University. Block of lockers in reading room.

South Dakota, University
of South Dakota. Lockers in
the stacks.

Tennessee, Vanderbilt University. On each stack level,
in same location, is a group
of lockers. A good arrangement.

Washington, D.C., George-
town University. Blocks of
lockers in bookstacks, near
carrels.

D.   FACULTY RESEARCH STUDIES

The practice of providing small rooms for faculty members working on research projects is widespread.

Architectural Intent

1. To locate studies near books but in a place designed to discourage interruptions by visitors.

2. To determine the right size. Practice varies from 48 square feet to 120 square feet.

3. To provide basic equipment — desk, bookshelves, typing table, and lounge chair.

California, University of California at Los Angeles. The usual location for faculty studies is along outer wall of bookstack area.

California, University of California at San Diego. Rather large rooms for research projects.

California, University
of California at Santa Cruz.
Small groups of boxes containing two to four studies,
at ends of stack ranges.

Canada, University of
Waterloo. Instead of placing
faculty studies along outer
wall, Waterloo places them
in a group in a module. No
outside windows.

Colorado, Colorado State
University. Six carrels per
room. Occupants must keep
a log and non-use results in
ejection. No shelf space.

England, East Anglia University. Engineer's spacing. Two studies per module along outer wall.

England, Essex University. Reader faces window, requiring venetian blind to keep out glare. Turning the table ninety degrees would help.

England, Warwick University. Well arranged study, but too much glare from window.

England, York University.
A double study. British are
accustomed to living in close
quarters.

England, York University.
An important person to rate
a single room.

Florida, Florida Southern
College. Small but
adequate.

Florida, University of Florida, Law Library. Generous table space. No outside window.

Florida, University of Florida, Law Library. Placement of faculty studies along inner wall next to books.

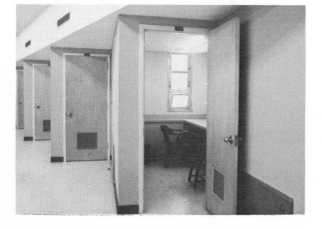

Florida, Jacksonville University. Saw-tooth exterior wall permits good small rooms.

Florida, Jacksonville University. Outside wall for faculty studies.

Georgia, Emory University. Generous and well planned space. File drawer below.

Georgia, University of Georgia, Science Library. Small but adequate (forty-eight square feet).

Germany, University of Frankfurt. Partitions about five feet high. No smoking.

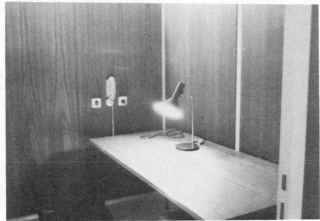

Germany, Stuttgart University. Notice telephone. Simple but adequate.

Illinois, Northwestern University. Well equipped, generous work space.

Indiana, Indiana University.
Well equipped and gen-
erous in size — approxi-
mately fifty-six feet.

Iowa, Luther College. Has
the essentials. Flat table.
Shelf. Typing stand and
electrical outlet.

Iowa, University of Northern Iowa. Group of faculty
studies in fairly secluded
location.

Louisiana, Tulane University. Glass partition top increases light supply. Note details of light fixtures.

Louisiana, Tulane University. Interior of study. Very generous.

Massachusetts, Amherst College. Good size and well equipped.

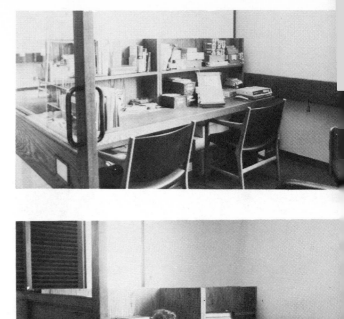

Massachusetts, Harvard
University, Countway Med-
ical Library. Shared by
two. Heavily used and much
in demand.

Massachusetts, Harvard
University, Countway Med-
ical Library. Same sized
room as above for students
and others.

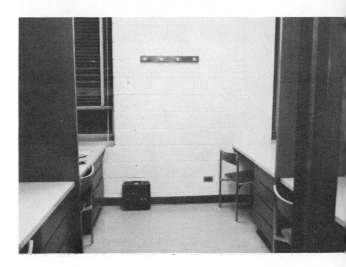

Michigan, Michigan Tech-
nological University. Four-
place faculty study.
Economical of space but
disliked by many professors
who prefer to work alone.

Minnesota, University of Minnesota. Places some faculty studies at edge of reading rooms rather than bookstacks.

Missouri, University of Missouri at Rolla. Nicely appointed studies. Note lighted shelf.

Missouri, University of Missouri at Rolla. This one is for the president. Note in-and-out letter rack and telephone!

Missouri, Washington University. Placement of studies along outer wall of bookstacks — reading room area.

Missouri, Washington University. Interior of study.

Nebraska, University of Nebraska, Home Economics Library. Two-place studies — director of libraries posing as scholar!

New York, Cornell University. Well organized. Note tack board.

New York, Rochester University. Placement of studies on edge of reading room.

New York, Rochester University. Interior of study. Shelves behind chair.

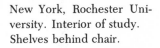

New York, State University of New York at Albany. Alcove of faculty study with student carrels in center. Note how architect used light fixture. No noise or smoking possible here.

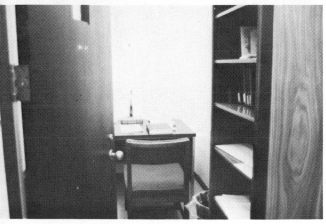

New York, State University of New York at Albany. Interior of study. No exterior window.

North Carolina, Duke University. Finely designed studies.

Ohio, John Carroll University. A block of faculty studies next to stacks.

Ohio, Ohio Northern University. Serrated arrangement along wall permits good room layout. A nice arrangement.

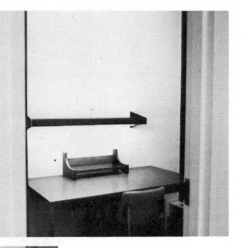

Ohio, Ohio Northern University. Interior. Simple but adequate.

Oklahoma, University of Oklahoma. A fairly permanent resident — a bibliographer!

Oregon, Portland State College. Nice, small studies.

Pennsylvania, Bryn Mawr
College. Generous work
space. Room for lots of
books. New building not yet
fully occupied at time
picture was taken.

Pennsylvania, Bryn Mawr
College. Groups of faculty
studies in inner module.
Secluded location.

Pennsylvania, Lehigh Uni-
versity, Science Library.
Nice studies. Carpeted.
Good fenestration. Lounge
chair.

Rhode Island, Brown University. Well designed. Ledge has lower section for typewriter.

Scotland, Glasgow University. A two-place study with lots of shelving space.

South Carolina, Clemson University. Clemson places about twenty carrels in a large room. Faculty opinion of this system depends on what type of study the faculty had used before.

South Dakota, University of South Dakota. A two-place study.

South Dakota, University
of South Dakota. Placement
of faculty studies around
edge of reading room.

Tennessee, Scarritt College.
A fairly large study. Bookshelf is a bit far from desk.

Texas, Southern Methodist
University, Science Library.
A large, well designed
room, long bench as work
space.

Washington, Eastern Washington State College. A properly designed study.

Washington, D.C., Georgetown University. Quite large and well equipped for studies!

Wisconsin, Beloit College. Long bench without provision for typewriter. No windows.

Wisconsin, University
of Wisconsin at Milwaukee.
Placement of studies at end
of reading room.

E.   SEMINARS

In the older German universities each faculty, or department, had its own research collection in its own quarters — and many still do. When the large American university libraries were built around the turn of the century, rooms for this kind of collection were included in the central library — usually on the top floor (Columbia, Minnesota, Michigan, North Carolina, Illinois, Oberlin). There was usually one seminar room for each humanities and social sciences department. Access was restricted to graduate students; and while seminar sessions were being held, no one could use the books.

Because of these handicaps and also because the seminar sessions usually ceased to make use of the collections in the rooms, after World War II universities incorporated the collections in the research stacks and allowed the rooms — *sans* books — to be used for graduate seminar sessions and books to be taken into the rooms as they were needed.

This system works for most but not all departments. The classics and particularly the classical archaeology departments yearn for the good old days when "their" books were all in one room and they did not have to chase all over the stacks to find them. Librarians have resisted going back to the old ways because they know a good deal of use is made of "their" books that the department faculties know little about.

But obviously the departments have a point and so some libraries have tried, without much success, to identify the core collections for each department that might be pulled out of the research stacks and placed as units for the convenience of faculty and graduate students — a concept that has been put into action for the undergraduates or lower division level students.

A close look at the seminar collections that exist at libraries like Cornell University, Bryn Mawr College, etc. suggests that more study of the problem is needed.

Another approach to this problem is to provide each department with a small lounge or club room with books in it that belong to the department, not the library, on the assumption that what the faculties really want is a place of their own to which they can escape from the impersonality of the large bookstack. The University of Colorado has done this, but no one would claim that it is either a success or a failure.

Architectural Intent

1. To place the seminars where noise from traffic will not bother readers.

2. To equip the seminars for full use of electronic communication and learning devices.

California, Chabot College. Room large enough for twenty-five but can be divided. Equipped for audio-visual use.

England, East Anglia University. For about fifteen people.

Florida, Florida Southern
College. T-shaped table for
about fifteen.

Iowa, Luther College. For
six. Closer to group study
room concept. Note audio-
visual outlets in rear.

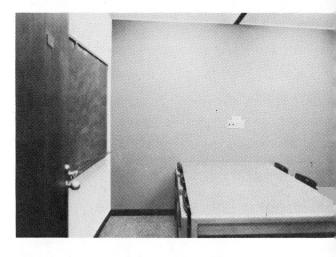

Kansas, Mt. St. Scholastica
College. Large room for
twenty.

Kansas, St. Benedict's College. Table for six to eight.

Massachusetts, Tufts University. Seats ten to twelve.

Michigan, Central Michigan University. Room for eight or ten.

Minnesota, University
of Minnesota. Table for ten.

Missouri, University
of Missouri at Rolla. For
fifteen to twenty people.
TV reception.

Nebraska, University of Nebraska, Agriculture Library.
For ten. Notice one side
opens onto central atrium.

New York, Cornell University. Seats ten. Trend is drifting back to permanent collections (all duplicates) with graduate seating for ten to twenty.

New York, State University of New York at Albany. Seats ten. Ventilation apparently not adequate.

Oregon, Reed College. Room capable of being divided.

Pennsylvania, Bryn Mawr
College. Room for 1,000
books and carrels for about
fifteen people in each
seminar room.

Pennsylvania, Lafayette
College. Table for eight to
ten.

Pennsylvania, Lehigh Uni-
versity, Science Library.
Seats ten.

Rhode Island, Brown University. Could seat up to twenty.

Scotland, Glasgow University. A new trend for central libraries in Britain. Seats fifteen to twenty.

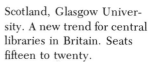

Wisconsin, Beloit College. A nicely appointed room for twelve or fourteen.

GROUP STUDY ROOMS

Because students frequently like, or need, to work in small groups for purposes of discussion, special rooms, next to the reading rooms, are frequently provided. These vary in size from rooms seating four up to regular seminar rooms.

Architectural Intent

1. To place rooms close to reading rooms.
2. To provide black board and outlets for audiovisual equipment.

Delaware, University of Delaware. Just the right size for four people.

Illinois, University of Chicago. Large enough to be used as seminar, as in this picture. No small group study rooms in this building.

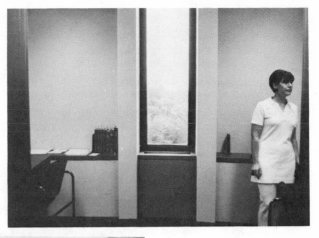

Illinois, Northwestern University. Rooms contain two carrels for study, but can be used as group study rooms. Note good fenestration.

Illinois, Northwestern University. Rooms for four.

Indiana, Indiana University, Research Library. Four people at individual tables.

Indiana, Indiana University,
Research Library. View
of series of group study
rooms.

Indiana, Notre Dame Uni-
versity. Central table for
four.

Iowa, Luther College. Seats
for six.

Iowa, University of Northern Iowa. Space for six.

Louisiana, Tulane University. A round table for four.

Massachusetts, Amherst College. A glass enclosed room near center of building for four.

Michigan, University
of Michigan, Undergraduate
Library. Room for four.

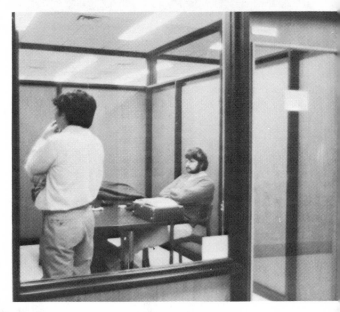

Minnesota, University
of Minnesota. For two
people.

New York, Wells College.
Room for two to four. This
building contains many interesting kinds of special
study places.

Oklahoma, University of Oklahoma. Room for four.

Pennsylvania, University of Pennsylvania, Wharton School. Group study rooms off central reference area near reserve desk.

Pennsylvania, Pittsburgh University. Room for four at end of reading room.

Tennessee, Fiske University. Two group study rooms
— each for two.

Texas, Abilene Christian
College. Group study room.

Texas, Rice University.
Room for four being used for
reading to blind.

Texas, University of Texas, Undergraduate Library. Room for four. These rooms are heavily used at Texas.

Utah, University of Utah. Somewhat larger than usual — for about six. Smoking permitted.

Utah, University of Utah. Room used for class project by library school students.

Washington, D.C., Georgetown University. Larger room, for six.

F.   FACULTY READING ROOMS

Older libraries in the United States sometimes followed the European custom of providing separate reading rooms for the faculty; but this is seldom done now because faculties do not wish to be separated, psychologically or physically, from students.

The practice is still common in law libraries (where customs die hard).

Florida, University of Florida, Law Library. Has duplicates of principal research sets, a luxury for the faculty. Seats for six to eight. Room is seldom used for reading. (See also University of Georgia Law Library.)

Colorado, University of Colorado. Philosophy reading room.

Two universities, however, have tried to develop departmental rooms to give each department a sense of "home base" in the library.

North Carolina, Duke University. Departmental room not yet occupied in new addition.

North Carolina, Duke University. A faculty lounge.

Missouri, Stephens College. Faculty offices in the library are uncommon — Stephens does provide some which draw students and faculty together.

G.   All-Night Study Rooms

Some institutions have provided special rooms that are kept open all night for students who, for several reasons, need these facilities.

Architectural Intent

1. To provide entrance to these rooms within the library during the daytime, but outside the rest of the library at night.

2. To meet code requirements in terms of access to toilets, fire escapes, etc.

Illinois, University of Chicago. Gate can be closed to block off rest of main floor. Entire reserve book area (large) becomes all-night study area. Supervision required.

Indiana, Earlham College. Room has its own entrance to left of library entrance. Entrance to rest of library is on right.

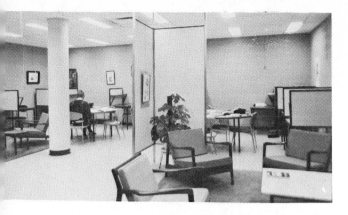

Indiana, Earlham College. Interior of room. No library books here. Just a place to study.

Minnesota, University of Minnesota. Provisions for overhead door to close off an area for all-night use if needed.

Pennsylvania, Lehigh University, Science Library. Study carrels. No library books. Has entrance from outside.

Washington, D.C., Georgetown University. Placed so that access from outside is possible.

H. Lounges and Smoking Rooms

All libraries make some provisions for readers who wish to read in a comfortable chair rather than study at a table or carrel. Variations in practice are great, both in numbers of such chairs and in their placement.

Architectural Intent

1. To place lounge areas where their informality does not clash, aesthetically, with the rest of the reading rooms.

2. If smoking is permitted, to provide adequate exhaust fans.

3. To provide a place for a reader's feet some place other than on adjacent chairs or tables.

California, University of California at Los Angeles, Research Library. Comfortable place to read while waiting for page to bring book from stacks. New bookshelves. Current periodicals room on right to rear.

Colorado, University of Colorado, Honors Library. Special lounge for honors students. Has small café at other end of room.

Florida, Florida Southern College. Lounge furniture near current periodicals.

Georgia, Emory University. Lounge furniture near current periodicals.

Georgia, University of Georgia, Science Library. A separate room for smoking.

Illinois, University of Chicago. Lounge area. Real comfort!

Illinois, University of Chicago. Lounge areas. Four chairs in each alcove.

Illinois, University of Illinois, Undergraduate Library. Much lounge furniture between bookshelves and atrium in center of building.

Indiana, Earlham College. A second lounge area in the middle of building.

Indiana, Indiana University. Lounge placed near entrance of undergraduate collections.

Indiana, Notre Dame University. Lots of lounge furniture distributed throughout library.

Iowa, Luther College. Lounge in corner of this building.

Iowa, University of Northern Iowa. A lounge for smoking in separate room.

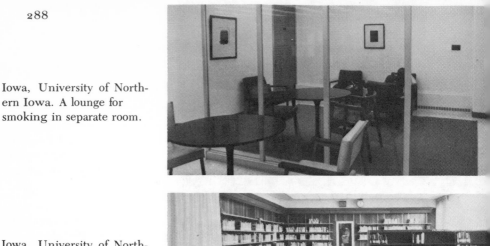

Iowa, University of Northern Iowa. Lounge area near new bookshelves.

Kansas, St. Benedict's College. Lounge corner with large window view of river and campus (to left). Picture taken at night.

Louisiana, Tulane University. Good lounge area near current periodicals. Note directory in front.

Massachusetts, Harvard University, Countway Medical Library. Rather formal lounge areas distributed throughout building.

Massachusetts, Harvard University, Radcliffe College. The poetry lounge.

Michigan, Central Michigan University. Lounge area near circulation desk and entrance to room.

Michigan, Grand Valley State College. Furniture at end of current periodicals shelves. Note "brain broiler" lighting.

Minnesota, University of Minnesota. On each reading room level at end of room is a smoking lounge.

Minnesota, University of Minnesota. Adjacent to reserve reading room is large smoking lounge.

Missouri, Stephens College. Lounge area at front of building separated from traffic by screens.

Missouri, Washington University. Lounges at corner of building on each floor.

Missouri, Washington University. Students do take good care of beautiful surroundings. Shoes on floor.

New York, Cazenovia College. A small group near periodicals.

New York, State University of New York at Albany. The building is full of lounge furniture. (See the Amenities.)

North Carolina, Duke University. Browsing groups dispersed throughout reading area.

North Carolina, University
of North Carolina, Under-
graduate Library. Lounge
furniture near central core
of building. Two chairs used
as improvised bed!! A
Monday morning.

Ohio, Bowling Green Uni-
versity. A nice area not far
from building entrance.

Ohio, John Carroll University. Smoking room at end
of reading room.

Ohio, John Carroll University. Lounge furniture in
Fine Arts room; attractive.

Oregon, Portland State College. There is an area like this near the entrance to each floor, each one slightly different in decor.

Pennsylvania, Kutztown State College. One end of a reading room.

Pennsylvania, Lafayette College. A nice area. Floor lamps help.

Pennsylvania, Lehigh University. Furniture placed along outside wall.

Pennsylvania, University
of Pennsylvania. The class of
'37 lounge area. Again,
shoes on floor.

Pennsylvania, University
of Pennsylvania, Wharton
School. The Peck lounge on
main reading room floor.

Pennsylvania, Pittsburgh
University. Smoking lounge
— enclosed. Part of browsing rooms on main floor.

Rhode Island, Brown University. Lounge furniture placed along "framed view."

South Carolina, Clemson University. Furniture at end of reading room.

South Dakota, University of South Dakota. Near front of the main floor. New bookshelf. Campus view when drapes not drawn.

Tennessee, Scarritt College. Front lounge, to right as you enter. Current periodicals.

Texas, Southwestern University. On second floor overlooking campus.

Texas, Southwestern University. A fireplace reading pit on main floor opposite entrance.

Texas, University of Texas, Undergraduate Library. A nice corner on each floor level.

Washington, D.C., George-
town University. Lounge
furniture placed in center
of building near bookstacks.

Wisconsin, University
of Wisconsin at Madison,
Agriculture Library.
Lounge furniture distrib-
uted on both levels. Here is
main floor.

Wisconsin, University of
Wisconsin at Madison, Medical Library. Lounge area
overlooking campus. At end
of stack area.

I. Typing Facilities

Even though students now use Xerox-type machines to make copies of library materials, they still use typewriters extensively for other reasons.

Architectural Intent

1. To provide facilities that will contain the noise.
2. To provide adequate shelf space for spreading out materials.

Florida, Jacksonville University. Group of typing carrels placed where noise will not bother readers.

Florida, University of Tampa. At end of smoking room is small room with four typing carrels. Good arrangement.

Georgia, Emory University. Small rooms for two typists.

Georgia, University of Georgia, Science Library. Room with typing booths on both sides.

Minnesota, University of Minnesota. Individual typing rooms, insulated.

Ohio, Ohio Northern University. Typical of rooms with many machines.

Pennsylvania, Pittsburgh University. Typing carrels with some sound proofing.

South Carolina, Clemson
University. A good layout.

Utah, Brigham Young Uni-
versity. Room with six to
eight typing machines.

Contemporary Furniture, University of California, Los Angeles

VI

Housing Books
and Other Media

NATURE OF THE PROBLEMS

1. Book collections are now growing so rapidly — in some areas doubling every three years, in most areas every ten years — that library buildings have to be expanded regularly.

2. Printed books no longer are the only carrier for information. Phonograph records and tapes, microforms, video tapes, computer tapes, etc. now have to be housed.

3. Readers want to get in the bookstacks and do their work near the materials they are reading. Housekeeping problems become formidable.

4. Shifting from multi-tier, self-supported bookstacks to modular buildings creates new freedoms and new restrictions. The multi-tier stack system was abandoned for three reasons: the columns could not be fireproofed, the system could not accommodate large numbers of readers working among the books, and the stacks were not adaptable to other uses when not needed for book storage.

Modular libraries permitted the shelving of books anywhere in the buildings and a mixture of books and reader stations. This created two kinds of problems.

a. Coherence. If readers are to find the block of bookstacks, or the specific books they want quickly, the bookstack ranges have to be arranged in such a manner that the sequence of classification numbers is easy to follow and is not interrupted by physical barriers, unusual layouts of ranges, too many oases, alcoves for readers, or other interruptions.

b. Expansion. The expansion problem arises from the fact that a book collection grows not solely at the end of the classification sequence but, like a sponge absorbing water, at all points in the sequence. Thus, room for newly-acquired books has to be left on each shelf of each range. When a given block of bookstack ranges is entirely full and a new one is to be occupied, all the books in the first unit will have to be shifted. There is no way of avoiding that. In a large university this is costly and annoying to the readers.

To minimize the cost and annoyance, provisions for expansion are planned so that space for new bookstack ranges can be made available immediately adjacent to the existing ranges without physical interruptions.

Thus:

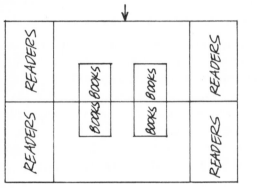

1st unit

2nd unit

5. Special storage facilities. Thus far librarians have assumed it was their duty to keep all books under their charge on the shelves in their original condition, instantly *accessible* to readers upon demand. Minor attempts to solve the *space* aspect (and therefore its accompanying *cost* aspect) have been sought through the storage of little-used materials in compact and allegedly less expensive quarters — sometimes on an inter-institutional cooperative basis — and through ordering certain materials as microforms. Both have had the effect of minimizing the accessibility of the publications to readers.

A new approach to management of the problem is being discussed by a few librarians under the label of "collections management" through the use of extensive knowledge of how readers work and accurate records of the use profile of each publication in the library.

Armed with these tools, librarians would no longer assume that their responsibility ended when they placed books on shelves, provided catalogs showing where each book belonged, and provided circulation systems that told who possessed books in use. Using the computer to provide the catalog of the collection as well as the records of its use (see the Ohio State University system), librarians would be able to house each publication in the place, in the form, and at the cost level best suited to each publication. Some would be housed in heavily-used college, undergraduate or course-related libraries; some in research-centered buildings; some in inexpensive or highly-compacted storage quarters; some in inter-institutional coordinated storage quarters; some reduced to microforms; and some recorded in computer data banks and preserved in their original format at perhaps only one place in the country.

National networks of bibliographical controls based on national library records of holdings of the nation's libraries, as well as financially subsidized facsimile transmission systems and computer networks based on various kinds of data banks, are all technologically possible today; but financially not viable.

Although prototype examples of the new approaches to the problem of growth have existed for some time (Ellsworth, Fussler, Morse, etc.) librarians have not been able, for a variety of reasons, to put them together into a massive program that would solve the growth problem in major ways.

When they do so, it will not be difficult to translate the architectural implications into actual building plans. Thus, an examination of the current scene will be useful not only for long-range but also for immediate planning.

When compact storage systems have been used, they are usually placed on the basement floor because of the heavy floor loads they impose. If the Randtriever system is to be used, a space some 25 feet high and 100 feet long and as wide as is needed should be provided so as to make maximum use of the system. It should be remembered that in selecting the appropriate storage system, the most efficient in terms of use of space is likely to be the most expensive in terms of cost per volume stored. Also, care should be taken to select the system that meets the institution's specific requirements. Some guidance on these matters can be found in the Ellsworth book on storage but since many of the systems described in that volume had not been installed at the time of writing, it would be wise to visit an actual installation. Each manufacturer, presumably, could furnish a list.

Pneumatic tube delivery systems between buildings can be seen at the Library of Congress, the University of California at Los Angeles, and Yale.

A. BOOKS — MANAGEMENT AND USE

California, University of California at Santa Cruz. Carrels along inner wall of courtyard. Books in nine-foot ranges. A few tables and lounge chairs at beginning of stack area.

California, University of California at Santa Cruz. Current journals and books with tables among blocks of ranges.

California, Chabot College. A community college. Round building. Books and carrels on mezzanine. Blocks of carrels on main floor.

England, University of Birmingham. Blocks of ranges on one side. Reading alcoves on the other.

England, University of Birmingham, Undergraduate Library. Area corresponding to our college or undergraduate libraries. Small book collection at side of room.

England, University of East
Anglia. Tables and carrels
along outside walls with book
ranges in middle.

England, Essex University.
Carrels with no side dividers
along outer walls. Books in
middle. Note light fixture.
Can be hung in either direction under exposed ceiling.

England, Sussex University.
Blocks of bookstacks with
various kinds of reader facilities among the blocks.

England, Warwick University. Carrels along outer wall of long reading room. Note light fixtures. Legible book range labels.

England, York University. Tables along outer walls. English architects use cylinder and spot lights too.

England, York University. Tables among the ranges.

England, York University. Reader stations along edges of atrium, next to books.

Florida, Florida Southern College. Books, typing carrels and reading room carrels. Note wooden baffles below large fluorescent light fixture.

Florida, Florida Technological University. Tables next to bookstacks.

Florida, University of Florida, College of Law. Unusual arrangement for a law library. Tables and carrels around a block of bookstack ranges.

Florida, University of Florida, College of Law. On other side of book ranges carrels only. A different type of light fixture used in this area.

Florida, University of Tampa. Three types of reader stations along book ranges. Note that light fixtures run at right angles to the stacks.

Florida, University of Tampa. A mixture of reader stations near books.

Florida, University of Tampa. A few tables placed in a module until space is needed for books.

France, Aix-en-Provence University, Droit Library. Large high-ceilinged reading room separated from book-stacks.

France, University of Nice, Science Library. Books form a spine along center of building — undergraduate readers on one side, graduates on the other.

France, University of Nice, Science Library. Opposite side of spine. Books above balcony.

Georgia, University of Georgia, Science Library. Tables and carrels among books.

Georgia, University of Georgia, Science Library. Same, but with lounge area near current periodicals.

Germany, University of Frankfurt. Reference books at one end of room with tables. Books are shelved under mezzanine containing current issues of periodicals.

Germany, Giessen University. Readers next to books and also on balcony. Bookstacks are not open to students.

Germany, Stuttgart University. Tables among the books.

Germany, Stuttgart University. Use of alcoves and mezzanines. Corridor is to left of bookcase running parallel to outer wall.

Germany, Stuttgart University. A special light fixture attached to reading room tables.

Illinois, University of Illinois, Undergraduate Library. Two types of reader stations among three kinds of bookshelves. Listening carrels in rear of room.

Illinois, Northwestern University. Three carrels were placed among radial stacks. In other alcoves five carrels and no low cases were used.

Iowa, University of Northern Iowa. Readers have choice of tables or carrels near books. Note that light fixture does not extend to wall where carrels are placed.

Massachusetts, Amherst College. Carrels, stacks. Faculty study at end of range.

Massachusetts, Harvard University, Lamont Library. The first modern use of alcoves. Note that readers would be working in a goldfish bowl.

Massachusetts, Harvard University, Radcliffe College. Tables in alcove.

Massachusetts, Harvard
University, Radcliffe College. Faculty member in
lounge chair in alcove.

Massachusetts, Harvard
University, Radcliffe College. Carrels next to stacks.

Massachusetts, Tufts Uni-
versity. Carrels near stacks.
Similar to Radcliffe.

Michigan, Central Michigan
University. A group of
four kinds of reader stations
with ranges on either
side.

Michigan, Eastern Michigan University. Books, carrels, group study rooms along outer walls.

Michigan, Grand Valley State College. Three kinds of reader stations at ends of ranges of books. Note change in ceiling height to provide for ventilation ducts.

Michigan, Northern Michigan University. Carrels along outer walls. Tables in shallow alcoves.

Michigan, Northern Michigan University. Tables and carrels in center of library.

Minnesota, University
of Minnesota. Tables and
carrels next to books.
Smoking lounge in back-
ground.

Missouri, University
of Missouri at Rolla. Lounge
furniture at ends of ranges.

Missouri, Stephens College.
A conventional layout —
blocks of stacks and blocks
of reader stations.

Missouri, Washington
University. Tables
and low cases.

Nebraska, University of Nebraska, Agriculture Library. On the mezzanine. Carrels next to atrium. Louverall light fixtures, with plastic lens under bulbs.

Nebraska, University of Nebraska, Agriculture Library. Same but under the eight-foot wide mezzanine opening.

New York, Rochester University. Tables and lounge furniture in alcove among stack ranges.

New York, State University of New York at Albany. Carrels at ends of ranges. Unusual lighting.

North Carolina, Elon College. Tables and carrels at ends of ranges.

Ohio, Findlay College. Carrels and tables in alcoves.

Ohio, John Carroll University. Mixture of four kinds of reader stations next to books.

Ohio, Ohio Northern University. Tables and carrels around block of bookstacks.

Oregon, Oegon State University. Tables in stack area.

Oregon, Oregon State University. Large area formally arranged.

Oregon, Portland State College. Mixture of reader facilities next to stacks.

Oregon, Reed College. In new addition, tables with dividers were placed next to stacks.

Oregon, Southern Oregon College. Tables on one side, carrels on the other.

Pennsylvania, Bryn Mawr College. Three kinds of facilities next to stacks. Note that ranges run parallel to wall, providing fewer points of access to books than does the usual plan.

Pennsylvania, Haverford College. In special reading room. Series of alcoves with books and readers above and below balcony.

Pennsylvania, Temple University. Temple placed blocks of stacks and reader facilities in checkerboard arrangement.

Rhode Island, Brown University. Two-place carrels in stack alcove.

Scotland, Edinburgh University. In large reading areas, rows of stacks are used to break up areas.

South Carolina, Clemson University. Carrels and tables next to books. Note type of light fixture in exposed ceiling pane.

South Dakota, University
of South Dakota. Tables
placed in stack module.

Tennessee, Austin Peay State
College. End view of com-
bined reading and bookstack
area.

Tennessee, Vanderbilt University. Books in block
ranges. Tables and carrels.

Texas, University of Texas,
Undergraduate Library.
Tables next to books.

Utah, University of Utah.
Tables and carrels with faculty
studies at end of room.

Wisconsin, Beloit College.
An "oasis."

Wisconsin, University
of Wisconsin at Milwaukee.
Carrels next to books.

Wyoming, University
of Wyoming. Tables and
carrels with locked boxes
in rear in stacks.

1. Bookshelves

a. Shelf Heights

Most American universities purchase bookstacks that have seven shelves on the average because the average reader cannot reach books on the eighth shelf. Some libraries use taller stacks with upper shelves for storage.

Florida, University of Florida. Uses eight shelves. University of Iowa also uses stack columns that will take eight shelves. Foot stools are necessary in these libraries.

Scotland, Glasgow University. Ranges six shelves high. Not uncommon in Great Britain.

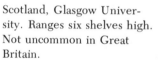

Pennsylvania, University of Pittsburgh. Uses columns that will take ten shelves. These are used at Pittsburgh to house manuscript boxes. Brown University uses the same idea in the lower stack levels for ultimate expansion. See also Chapter on expansion in Brown University and Clemson.

b. *End Panels and Guides*

To dress up the appearance of bookstacks, end panels are frequently used. One library goes further and has decorated end panels in its main reading room.

Texas, Southern Methodist.

England, Warwick University. Two libraries, Warwick in England and Emory in the United States, have done an excellent job of putting guides at ends of ranges large enough to show contents of range. Note also Warwick's use of range face for display.

c. *Inspection Shelves*

Individuals using a bookstack need a place to rest a book while inspecting it to see if they want to take it to a table. Typical kinds of inspection shelves are presented.

Georgia, Emory University. Emory provides a low book-case every fourth range. The top of case can be used as table top.

Pennsylvania, University of Pennsylvania. Pennsylvania simply leaves one vacant shelf at proper height at end of each range.

Illinois, Northwestern University. Pull-out shelf on which to rest a book at hip level.

Texas, Abilene Christian College. Reading shelf is placed in center of outside face of block of stacks — impossible to do within a block unless aisles were widened.

Texas, Rice University. Sturdy pull-out shelves for reference book use. These are wooden cases.

Washington, Pacific Lutheran University. Uses pull-out shelf at ends of ranges for inspection purposes. Jack Haley, librarian, demonstrating shelf.

d. *Oversizes*

California, University of California at Los Angeles. One type using regular shelves placed close together. Books on side. Larger books can be placed flat extending through both sides of range. See University of Minnesota.

Minnesota, University of Minnesota. Large volumes are placed vertically here extending through both sides of ranges. Top two shelves on right hold books on their sides extending through both sides.

Ohio, Bowling Green University. Special bracket shelves for wide books.

e. *Placement of Book Cases*

Most libraries place stack ranges in rows with a thirty-inch aisle between the ranges. For storage libraries the aisle is sometimes as small as twenty-one inches. The ranges vary from three to twenty-seven feet long, or even longer in special cases. In a large bookstack, four-foot lateral aisles are located around the stack blocks and down through the center to take care of book truck passage.

To avoid the monotony of the typical stack, several types of stack placement have been tried.

Illinois, Northwestern University, radial stack. Fourteen inches between stack ends. It is hard to use books in first two sections. At other end, there's more space than needed.

Illinois, Northwestern University. Placing carrel in radial stacks helps use excessive space, but creates traffic problem.

Illinois, Northwestern University. Radial layout tends to force circulation layout for other pieces of equipment. Here are vertical file cases.

New York, Wells College.
Radial stacks. At wide end
of radial stacks space is excessive. Also, problems of
reader orientation.

Texas, Abilene Christian
College. Stacks placed at
forty-five degree angle.

Compact Stacks. There are some twelve kinds of compact storage systems in use, or available for use. (See Ralph E. Ellsworth, *The Economics of Book Storage*, The Association of Research Libraries and The Scarecrow Press, Inc., Metuchen, New Jersey, 1969. Also, Drahoslav Gawrecki, *Compact Library Shelving*, American Library Association, Chicago, Illinois, 1968.)

Arizona, University
of Arizona, The Stor-Mor
drawer type of compact
stacks made by Ames Book-
stack Company. Can be
installed in multi-tier bookstack, as done here.

England, York University.
A Compactus installation in
storage room.

New Jersey, Princeton University. Princeton has a separate storage building. Books are arranged in eight size groups and are stored by classification number with the call numbers showing. Aisles are narrow — twenty-two inches. Not a browsing environment but adequate for storage.

New York, Randtriever. A prototype installation at factory. Computer controlled console in foreground. Bookstack ranges in background. Delivery chutes between.

Sweden, Chalmers Technical University. Compactus installation. Used frequently in Great Britain and on continent. Japanese version is marketed in United States under name of Elecompack.

Texas, Rice University. Manually controlled Compactus system used for storing manuscript boxes and some books in rare book room.

Washington, D.C., American University. Elecompack installation. Looking into aisle between cases. Notice rails on floor and placement of light fixture for each aisle.

Wisconsin, University of Wisconsin at Milwaukee. Uses Hamilton drawer system. University of Michigan at Ann Arbor uses Ames drawer system. University of Arizona uses Ames system for government documents; Illinois State University at Normal uses it for microforms and books.

2. Book Handling

In small libraries books are moved by means of book trucks and elevators. For large libraries there are several kinds of mechanical systems.

a. Conveyors

American conveyors have one delivery point per floor. The European Siemens system has a trough just below the bookstack ceiling containing a continuously moving belt. The page takes the book from the shelf, places it on the belt and the conveyor delivers it to the desk.

California, University of California at Los Angeles, Research Library. Pneumatic tube station and book conveyor delivery point.

California, University of California at Santa Barbara. Samson book conveyor delivery chute on top floor of library.

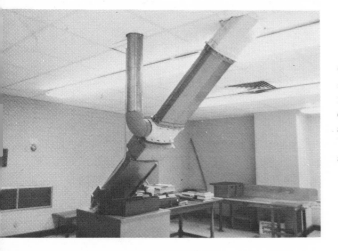

Connecticut, Yale University. Pneumatic tube system for delivering books to other buildings. Used also at Library of Congress and University of California at Los Angeles.

Holland, Delft Technological Institute. Spiral delivery
chute from top floors.

Germany, University of
Frankfurt. Belts bring book
to delivery desk.

Germany, University of Frankfurt. Belt can turn corner.

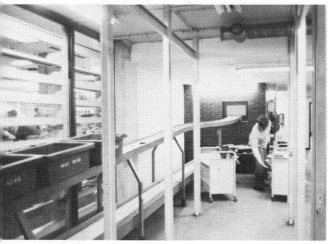

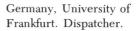

Germany, University of Frankfurt. Dispatcher.

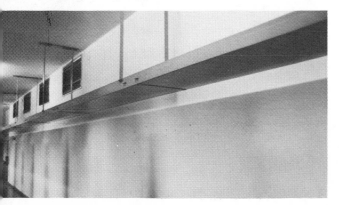

Germany, Stuttgart University. Conveyor trough suspended from ceiling.

Germany, Stuttgart University. Delivery chutes.

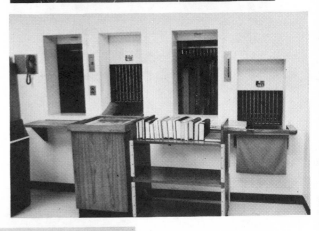

Illinois, University of Chicago. Book conveyor. System uses baskets instead of putting each book on a conveyor belt or cage basket attached to revolving chain.

Indiana, Indiana University. Book conveyor delivery point. Individual books are placed on moving conveyor belt.

Minnesota, University of Minnesota. Conveyor delivery chute.

b. *Book Return Chutes*

No library has solved the problem of providing after-hour book return systems that do not overflow and damage book bindings. Depressible-top book trucks placed under the return slots overflow and dump books on the floor if there is no one there to change trucks. A sloping chute that empties books onto a flat table is all right as long as the table does not fill up.

Minnesota, University of Minnesota. After hours, books are placed in a book return slot which empties onto inclined chute shown, then onto flat table at bottom. Books come open and break up during descent.

Oregon, University of Oregon, Science Library.
Roller system. Works well as long as books do not pile up.

c. *Communications with the Pages*

Various systems are used: pneumatic tubes for sending call slips; telephone messages; walkie-talkies. Several libraries use the Motorola portable radio system. (Brown University and Indiana University)

Indiana, Indiana University. Portable radio receiver carried by page in stacks.

Indiana, Indiana University. Radio control system on floor below. Messages are broadcast to pages from this desk.

3. *Book Protection*

a. *Bookstack Entrance Controls*

Closed stack libraries use a variety of methods of controlling the entrance to their bookstacks.

California, University
of California at Los Angeles.
Uses a lady sitting at a desk.

Georgia, Emory University.
Entrance to bookstacks.
Once beyond gate one has
access to elevators and stair
wells. "Main" floor of library (one level down)
containing keys is open to
everyone.

Georgia, Emory University.
Gate opens by student in-
serting I.D. card in control
slot on right. I.D. card is
also used at Boston University stack entrance.

Illinois, University of Chicago. Entrance to stacks. Permits required. Main floor is open to all.

Scotland, Edinburgh University. Before the new building was settled in, access to bookstacks was gained as the sign instructed, "Please ring vigorously for attention." Unfortunately the bell has been replaced.

Illinois, University of Chicago. Stack controls. Bookstacks open to all but books must be charged out as readers go from stack to reading rooms.

b. *Fire Protection*

It is generally believed that of the two traditional destroyers of books — fire and water — water is likely to do more damage unless the entire bookstack is consumed by fire. For this reason librarians favor a combination of a fire detection system and CO_2 fire extinguishers — portable ones in most parts of the library with automatic ones in rare book rooms. A new type that sprays a fine mist for a short time is being considered for the University of California at Berkeley.

Connecticut, Yale University, Beinecke Library. An installed CO_2 system in rare book room. An outlet is shown.

Rhode Island, Brown University. Control panel for fire detection system. Alarm also rings in campus security center.

Indiana, Indiana University. Fire detection unit in bookstacks.

England, York University. Fire detection unit.

Texas, Rice University, rare book room. This system requires a large battery of CO_2 containers. Similar installations at Yale and Princeton.

4. Rare Book Rooms

This report has, with one exception, concerned itself with rare book departments in central libraries only, not with separate rare book libraries as at Indiana and Harvard. This is such a highly specialized and personalized subject that it deserves a separate treatment.

Architectural Intent

1. To provide tight control over access to the rare books with provisions for readers that permit close supervision by the staff.

2. To provide correct temperature and humidity levels, dust filtering systems, and lighting systems that will not injure the paper and bindings of rare books.

California, California Institute of Technology. For very small or moderately restricted access, a simple system of bookstack cage panels is used.

Connecticut, Yale University, Beinecke Library. This interior view of separate rare book building is included to show one way of housing rare books and related study areas. Books are protected from contact with sunlight, excessive heat, dirt and low humidity. Photos by Ezra Stoller Associates, Rye, New York.

Florida, University of Florida. Rare book reading room with staff desks at one end and rare book stacks on other side of far wall.

Georgia, Georgia Institute of Technology. Within large rare book room is inner sanctum for china donated by family who furnished the room. Used as a meeting place for special people.

Illinois, University of Chicago. Rare book control: books are on one level below, staff can oversee readers in reading room. Staff work room and offices are on right side of desks. A good system.

Illinois, University of Illinois. Illinois has one of best rare book systems: three reading areas — one for exhibits, one for general public, one for users of manuscripts. This one is for general public. Staff rooms have glass walls for supervision.

Illinois, University of Illinois. Exhibit room, between room for general readers and room for specialists.

Illinois, University of Illinois. The third room — for scholars using manuscripts and rare books.

Iowa, University of Iowa. Iowa places its "Iowa Authors Collection" — heavily used — at front of rare book stacks.

Maryland, Johns Hopkins University. Small reading room with stacks below. Librarian's office is on left of table. Very nice.

Massachusetts, Amherst College. Small room with collection around wall, on main floor.

Massachusetts, Amherst College. This permits supervision of reading room.

Minnesota, University of Minnesota. Entrance to rare book area — a large and important system with controls similar to those at University of Illinois.

Minnesota, University of Minnesota. Librarian can supervise reading room.

Minnesota, University of Minnesota. Looking across reading room toward offices.

Missouri, Washington University. Librarians usually put manuscripts in boxes like these. Books are shelved in usual manner.

Missouri, Washington University. Exhibit cases within the rare book room are customary.

New York, Cornell University. Exhibit cases in rare book room lobby. Entrance through door in far corner.

New York, Cornell University. Entrance to rare book reading room controlled by girl at desk.

New York, Cornell University. Rare book librarian can supervise reading room. View from librarian's desk.

North Carolina, Duke University. Entrance to manuscript room. Librarian's office with glass walls. Entrance door on right of far wall.

North Carolina, Duke University. View of manuscript room from librarian's office with small rooms on opposite side for scholars.

North Carolina, Elon College. Small colleges frequently acquire rare books and objects to be preserved. Here it is china.

Ohio, John Carroll University. Another system of caging off an area of the bookstacks.

Oklahoma, University of Oklahoma. Impressive entrance to an important rare book collection.

Oklahoma, University of Oklahoma. The Degolyer reading room office is on left. Entrance to stacks on right.

Oklahoma, University of Oklahoma. Librarian can supervise reading room with rare book stacks visible beyond.

Oregon, Lewis and Clark University. Houses its rare books within rare book reading room.

Pennsylvania, Bryn Mawr
College. Special cases for
rare books.

Pennsylvania, Lafayette
College. Slightly more
formalized system is to
enclose rare books in glassed
area.

Scotland, Glasgow Uni-
versity. Glasgow's great rare
book collections are placed
on main level and housed
with dignity and care.

Scotland, Glasgow University. A view of Glasgow's rare book collections. The rarest books are in special cabinets on right.

Tennessee, Fiske University. Entrance to special collections room with manuscripts and records of Negro composers in background. An impressive room.

Tennessee, Fiske University. Special cases for rare phonograph records.

Tennessee, Scarritt College. Special cases for bibles. Screen door fronts for ventilation.

Texas, Rice University. Rare book readers use these desks. Adequate supervision from office.

Texas, Rice University. Details of desk. Also view of entrance and office. Door to stacks on right.

Texas, Southwestern University. Pleasant rare book room overlooking campus.

Utah, Brigham Young University. Special collections reading room is used heavily: less noisy than rest of library, nice furniture.

Washington, D.C., Georgetown University. Exhibit cases along wall. Control desk in rear. One table for readers.

Wisconsin, University of Wisconsin at Madison, Medical Library. A history of medicine corner in rare book room.

5. Pamphlets

Two systems are used for housing pamphlets: in folders in vertical files; and in pamphlet boxes on shelves.

Oregon, Oregon State University. Pamphlets in vertical file cases near reference area.

Canada, University of Waterloo. A second system is to put pamphlets in special boxes on bookshelves, either in one place or by classification number.

6. Maps and Atlases

Most libraries keep maps in drawers in cabinets.
Some use low cases with tops for reading maps. Others provide regular tables.

Canada, Guelph University. Tracing table between map cases, tops used for reading maps.

Delaware, University
of Delaware. Large collection. Top of low cases for
reading.

Georgia, Georgia Institute
of Technology. Large collection in well equipped room.

Georgia, University of Georgia, Science Library. Central case left low enough
for reading.

Idaho, University of Idaho.
All cases tall. Tables for
reading.

Illinois, Northwestern University. Sloping tops for reading maps.

Louisiana, Tulane University. Low cases.

Michigan, Central Michigan University. Tables for use. Cases high.

Minnesota, University of Minnesota. High cases. Tables for reading.

Oklahoma, University of Oklahoma. Tables for reading.

Oregon, Oregon State University. Well equipped map room.

Oregon, Portland State College. Tables for reading.

Rhode Island, Brown University. Two types of cases, one for maps, one for atlases.

Washington, D.C., George-
town University. Cases just
behind card catalog for
atlases.

Wisconsin, University
of Wisconsin at Milwaukee.
Hanging rack.

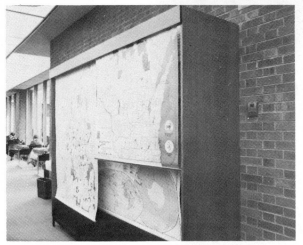

B.   OTHER MEDIA

1. Listening

California, Chabot College.
Control console in fore-
ground, listening carrels in
background. A few rooms
with individually controlled
record and tape players in
background.

California, Chabot College.
Tape desk console.

California, Chabot College.
Dial access system. Attendant plays a tape, listener
plugs in earphones.

California, Chabot College.
Students request specific
tape by dialing its number.
Close-up of listening carrels.

California, Stanford University, Undergraduate Library. Listening center. Control room in background. Units mostly dial access but some individually controlled units.

California, Stanford University, Undergraduate Library. Close-up of listening units for records and tapes.

California, Stanford University, Undergraduate Library. Students use carrels distributed through building to plug in earphones and listen to prescheduled programs. No individual control or selection.

California, Westmont College. Conventional record and tape players. Student checks out earphones and records and tapes, controls his own playing.

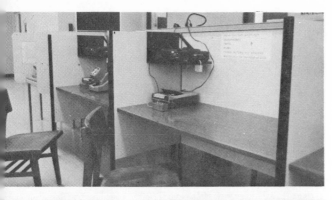

Colorado, University of Colorado, College Library. Individual record and tape players. Several dial access units connect with programs put on by audiovisual department in separate building. Earphones check out at reserve desk. Audiovisual listening equipment is provided.

Colorado, University of Colorado, College Library. Audiovisual listening.

Colorado, University of Colorado, Business Library. Video tape recorder.

Colorado, University of Colorado, Business Library. Cassettes for loop broadcasting system.

England, East Anglia University. Individually controlled players in tables. No dial access.

England, Warwick University. Individually controlled players. No dial access.

Illinois, University of Illinois, Undergraduate Library. Individually controlled players in room. Dial access equipment is provided in another area.

Illinois, University of Illinois, Undergraduate Library. Listening carrels with dial access. Control console in background.

Illinois, Northwestern University. Poetry listening room. Both dial access and individually controlled players.

Illinois, Northwestern University. Dial access carrels.

Indiana, Indiana University, Undergraduate Library. Individually controlled players only are available.

Iowa, University of Northern Iowa. Individually controlled players in separate room on main floor.

Kansas, Mt. St. Scholastica College. Individually controlled players in tables and in listening rooms behind.

Massachusetts, Boston University. Uses mostly dial access units with control console. But has a few individually controlled players.

Massachusetts, Harvard University, Radcliffe College. Individually controlled players.

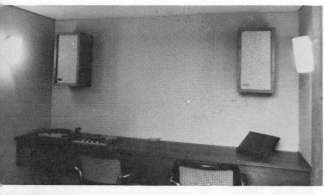

Massachusetts, Harvard University, Radcliffe College. Listening room with speakers. Individually controlled players.

Michigan, Central Michigan University. Individually controlled tape decks.

Michigan, University of Michigan, Undergraduate Library. Pre-scheduled tapes play from console for as many as 144 people at one time. A few individual record players exist. Dial access system expected to be outmoded by cassettes.

Michigan, Michigan Technological University. Individually controlled tape decks in small room.

Minnesota, University of Minnesota. Thirty-one persons can listen at one time to tape played from central console. No individual control.

Minnesota, University of Minnesota. Listening room tape recorder.

Missouri, University of Missouri at Rolla. Tape and record players.

Missouri, Stephens College. Individually controlled tape decks and dial access to control console in audiovisual building. Players for records available.

Missouri, Stephens College.
Tape players.

Missouri, Washington Uni-
versity. Individual players
in listening room. No dial
access.

New York, Rochester Uni-
versity. Console with
players, several can plug in.

New York, Wells College.
Individual players for records and tapes.

North Carolina, Elon Col-
lege. Individual players.

North Carolina, University
of North Carolina, Under-
graduate Library. Individual
players.

Ohio, John Carroll University. Listening rooms. All
individually controlled
players.

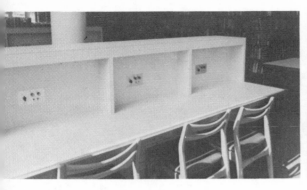

Oregon, Lewis and Clark
University. Dial access units.

Pennsylvania, Lafayette
College. Dial access carrels.

Pennsylvania, Temple Uni-
versity. Dial access system.

South Dakota, University of South Dakota. Individually controlled players.

Texas, Abilene Christian College. Audiovisual carrels.

Texas, Abilene Christian College. Audiovisual. Tape duplicator.

Texas, University of Texas, Undergraduate Library. Both dial access and individually controlled units.

Texas, University of Texas, Undergraduate Library. Close-up of units.

Utah, Brigham Young University. Two types of dial access units. A few individual players for records are kept in room.

Utah, University of Utah. Same system as at Brigham Young University.

Washington, Washington State University. Individual players.

Washington, Washington
State University. Individual players.

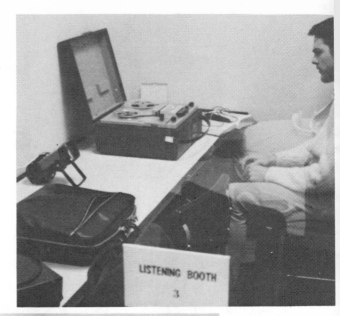

Washington, Washington
State University. Dial
access units.

2. *Looking*

California, Chabot College.
Seminar equipped for group
TV viewing.

England, East Anglia University. Individual video tape viewers. This is an exceedingly important machine. It does to video tapes what the cassette does to listening tapes.

Kansas, St. Benedict's College. Audiovisual room equipped for TV reception.

Kansas, St. Benedict's College. Seminar equipped for viewing.

Oklahoma, Oklahoma State University. Individual viewer for video tape.

Oklahoma, Oral Roberts
University. Carrels
equipped with TV receiv-
ers. Also dial access for
listening.

Oregon, Oregon Southern
College. Use of closed cir-
cuit TV camera to supervise
reading room.

Oregon, Oregon Southern
College. TV screen shows
patron waiting for attention
at desk outside.

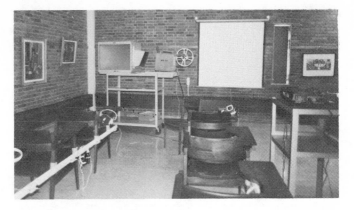

Missouri, Stephens College. Group viewing and listening from TV or motion picture screen. Earphones for each chair.

Washington, D.C., Georgetown University. A study wired for sound and TV reception.

Washington, D.C., Georgetown University. There are two rooms for group reception of films, etc.

3. Storage of Hardware for Listening, Viewing and Data Processing

California, Chabot College. Storage for film strip reels, tapes, cassettes, motion picture films — and headphones.

California, Chabot College. Storage for viewers and listening equipment.

California, University of California at San Diego, Medical Library. A "teaching machine."

California, Stanford University, Undergraduate Library. Tape deck console.

California, Stanford University, Undergraduate Library. Control room for language laboratory in library.

California, Stanford University, Undergraduate Library. Earphone storage at reserve desk.

Colorado, Colorado State University. Tapes on open shelves adjacent to carrels.

Illinois, University of Illinois, Undergraduate Library. Control room for listening equipment.

Illinois, Northwestern University. Tape deck console.

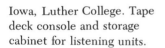

Iowa, Luther College. Tape deck console and storage cabinet for listening units.

Minnesota, University of Minnesota. Tape player console.

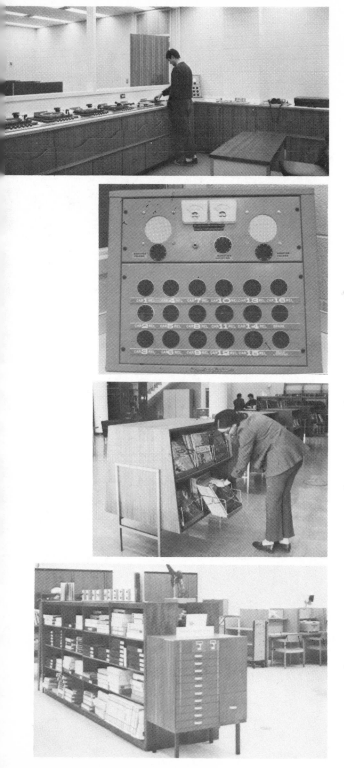

Missouri, St. Benedict's College. Record and tape player control desk.

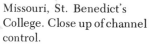

Missouri, St. Benedict's College. Close up of channel control.

Missouri, Stephens College. Phonograph record storage cabinets.

Pennsylvania, Pittsburgh University. Media shelf in curriculum laboratory.

384

South Dakota, University
of South Dakota. A teaching
machine.

Utah, Brigham Young Uni-
versity. Tape player console.

Utah, University of Utah.
Audiovisual desk on second
floor, showing tape deck
console.

Washington, Washington
State University. Tape and
record player console.

Washington, Washington State University. Reception and viewing room.

Washington, Washington State University. The graphics room.

Washington, Washington State University. Equipment in audiovisual work room.

Washington, Washington State University. Film storage bins.

Washington, Washington
State University. The repair
room.

C.   Microforms — Housing and Use

General Comments. Very few of the new libraries have made
major improvements in their provisions for microform use. The
machines are still placed on tables or in carrels with too little
space for notetaking, use of books, etc. The Donald C. Holmes
study for A.R.L. recommended several desirable carrels
(pp. 13–16) but none of this type was observed.

Issues

1. *Centralized versus Decentralized Use.*

Until the collections become very large, most libraries keep
the microforms in one place where staff supervision from some
other department is available — frequently the reference staff.
Since the area where the reading is done needs to have subdued
lighting, it is easier to do this in one separate room than it is
to disperse the facilities throughout the building, but both are
possible.

2. *Housing Microforms.*

Microforms are stored in many ways — in drawers, in cabinets,
on regular library shelves, and in trolleys. Thus far only one library
has used one of the compact or mechanized systems of storage,
such as Randtriever, but manual systems like those used at the
University of Minnesota are reasonably convenient and economical.

Humidity levels are usually kept above 40 percent and temperature ranges vary from sixty-five to seventy-five degrees. The
A.N.S.I. has recently issued standards for archival storage of microfilms. See bibliography.

3. *Facilities for Use.*

Readers need space to take notes while using microforms, and many prefer to use a typewriter, which is a source of noise annoyance in a library. Typing can create floor or furniture vibration that can damage filaments in the bulbs in the readers.

The M.I.T. Barker Library (a part of the Intrex project) will link a computerized bibliographical contact with the images on microfiche in such a manner that the reader will not only be able to read the image on a screen, but also to get a copy immediately.

The introduction of pre-loaded cassettes, now in its early stages, should eliminate the problems readers now have in feeding microfilm into the reading machines.

New portable microreaders are being introduced for microfiche; presumably these will become as common as portable typewriters.

Comments from microform users encountered in this study suggest that there are many unsolved problems associated with the use of microforms. None of these is, however, a matter of architecture.

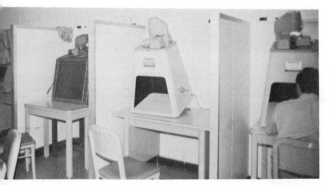

California, University of California at Los Angeles. Note lack of space for note taking, typewriters, etc.

California, Chabot College. Microreaders placed along a wall with note taking space between readers.

Colorado, Colorado State University. A view of room showing types of machines.

Colorado, Colorado State University. Microreaders in one room, placed on slightly sloping shelf. Rheostat control of overhead lighting.

Colorado, University of Colorado. Readers placed in darkened area in reading room carrels.

Colorado, University of Colorado. Microforms in drawers.

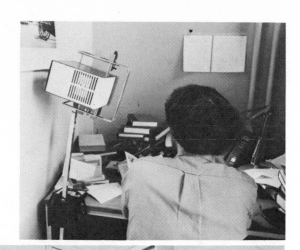

England, York University. New kind of microreader in faculty member's study projects image on wall. Student reported he liked it for freedom it gave him to move around while reading.

Florida, University of Florida. Reels stored in pull-out panels as well as in drawers.

Illinois, University of Chicago. Microfilm storage. Films in catalogues in boxes, shelved in movable ranges. One aisle for six or seven ranges.

Illinois, University of Chicago. Readers in darkened area on right. Counter next to control desk. Films behind desk — an excellent arrangement.

Maryland, Johns Hopkins University. Entrance to area. Microreaders in booths are large enough for typewriters.

Minnesota, University of Minnesota. Places microreaders in one room. A fair amount of work space.

Minnesota, University of Minnesota. Stores film reels in paper boxes — one box on side with one reel in it. Good system. Ten reels per box.

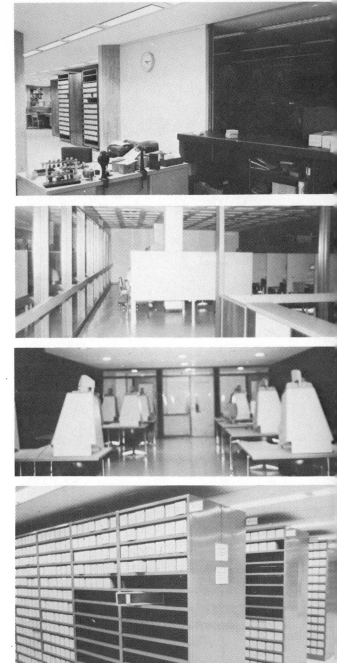

New York, Cornell University. Large area with micro-readers in darkened areas at edges of room.

New York, Cornell University. Microfilm area also includes map room. Micro-print boxes on left.

New York, Cornell University. Microfilm reels in paper boxes.

North Carolina, Duke University. Stores some microfilm in boxes.

Ohio, John Carroll University. Larger reading area adjacent to storage area.

Oregon, Oregon Southern College. Built special booths for microreaders. Little space for note taking.

Pennsylvania, Kutztown State College. This arrangement provides some work space.

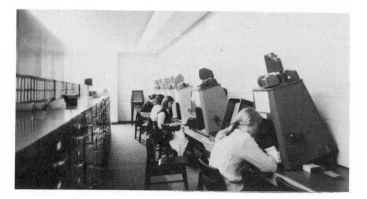

Rhode Island, Brown University. Each room provides good working space for note taking, etc.

Tennessee, Vanderbilt University. Micro storage area caged.

Washington, Eastern Washington State College. Places microforms and readers in regular reading room. Area must be darkened.

394

Washington, Pacific Lutheran University. Stores films in boxes classified and placed with books by subject. Possible in smaller libraries — could be done in any library.

Washington, Washington State University. Most large libraries need a camera for microfilming their own materials. Basic camera is shown.

Superior Microfilm Reader, Microfilms and Materials Company. One of newly designed carrels for microform reading. Space for taking notes. Screen can be tipped slightly. Cost: about $1200.

University of Northern Iowa

VII

Types of Libraries in Colleges and Universities

NATURE OF THE PROBLEM

IN most large colleges and universities, the entire library system is governed and managed as a unified system under the direction of the director of libraries. The law school libraries are sometimes governed separately, as are the medical school libraries if they are located in a separate city.

Departmental libraries usually occupy space in a departmental building rather than in a building of their own. This is not true of law and medical libraries, or of universities which have a separate science library.

When departmental libraries occupy space in a departmental building certain architectural issues exist:

1. Placing the library on the main floor of the building where it will be convenient for readers who come from other parts of the campus.

2. Placing the library so it can be used when the rest of the building is locked off.

3. Allowing room for expansion adjacent to the library.

4. Providing access from the building loading dock to a side door in the library.

5. Insulating the library from distracting activities going on in the rest of the building.

Except for the above needs, the planning of departmental libraries is the same as the planning of the general library. However, there are some specific needs associated with some types — such as special, wide shelves for oversized art books, slide cases and cabinets, and display wings in *art and architecture libraries*. In music libraries much highly specialized equipment is required (see section on music libraries.) *Medical libraries* differ little from other science libraries; they maintain a special section where "this week's" new journals are put — a practice that is also followed in science libraries.

Law school libraries present special problems to architects in that their planners seem to have successfully resisted most of the new concepts developed during the last twenty-five years to make libraries easier and more pleasant to use. The domination of the older generation of law school faculties, who insist that they know best how to plan law libraries, accounts for this lag. The two exceptions are to be found at the University of Florida Law School Library in Gainesville and the Southern Methodist University. New improvements are as follows:

First, placing the circulation desk outside the central reading room, with a glass wall between to keep the inevitable circulation desk noise from distracting the readers while not making it much more difficult for readers to ask the "where is it?" type of question. Second, reversing the position of books and readers so that readers do not have to sit in the middle of a gold fish bowl while studying. The idea of placing at least the bibliographic tools and other reference guides between the entrance and the central reading room has greatly improved law library reading room facilities. Third, the use of conference or group study rooms (for four to six people) adjacent to reading rooms has also been found to be convenient for students who wish to discuss matters with their fellow students. The University of California at Los Angeles has one such room in its law library.

Even though it is fairly obvious that a law school student will use a large number of books at any one time, the size of the carrel working space in law libraries does not usually reflect this need. A flat working space of 2-by-4 feet is minimal, while 2½-by-5 feet would not be extravagent. It should also be noted that seating space for 90 percent of the enrollment is normal. Also, because law students spend long periods of time studying, some have lounge furniture easily available for a change of reading posture. The European type of café where the needs of the inner man can be met is sometimes provided.

Usually if money is available, the architect will be expected to make the law library reflect the prestigious position and the grandeur of the law school by means of wood-paneled rooms and other architectural symbols of success.

The University of Houston Law School has provided, on the level below the main floor — which itself is underground — an entire floor of study carrels, six or eight to an alcove. Opinion as to the desirability of this arrangement is divided, with some negativism resulting from the smallness of the carrels and their distance from the book collections.

Some law schools provide a separate reading room for the faculty. The purpose of this is not clear — even to the law faculties, because each law faculty member almost always has a generous office — occasionally shared by a colleague. The idea of a faculty reading room is probably a carry-over from the late nineteenth century when most university libraries had such rooms. The ones I have inspected are either empty or haphazard in use.

On the other hand, small faculty research offices seem as useful to law faculties as to men in other parts of the university.

There is one more architectural habit in law libraries frequently seen, and that is the use of a mezzanine for current issues of periodicals. It is not clear just what law library readers have done to justify this penalty unless it forces them to get a little exercise and thus clear their minds. Nevertheless, it does seem that a more accessible (and frequently not so hot) location could be found for current periodicals. Other libraries do it.

Science libraries. In recent years the growing interdependence among the various science departments has suggested the wisdom of developing a single science library in which, with a minimum of running around, students and faculty will find the literature of all the sciences under one roof. Some of these (Southern Methodist University, Johns Hopkins, Georgia, Arizona, and Oregon) are in separate buildings. Some are underground or adjacent to science buildings (Yale and Oregon.) Some occupy one of the floor levels in the central library (SUNY at Albany) and several are in the planning stage (Harvard and Colorado.)

The underground location is appropriate where aboveground space is scarce, but care must be taken to make sure that expansion is possible.

There are about as many philosophies for organization of science libraries as there are for general libraries, but two conditions are clearly demanded. First, easy and quick access to current journals; and second, facilities for the use of computerized networks and services and for microform projects.

Architects should be aware of the rapid growth of science literature, and its habit of relating to the needs of semi-scientific disciplines in the university. The rapid obsolescence of older scientific literature has enabled science libraries to send to storage about the same amount of literature that is added each year, but not many have done this.

Music libraries. The following types of use are common to music libraries:

1. The casual listerner charging out books, records, and tapes. He sometimes wants to listen to the records first and for this purpose headphones with individual players are usually present.

2. Students listening to spoken word records and tapes and musical records and tapes for daily assignments. For the non-specialist, earphones give sufficient fidelity. Individual players give the listener the best control over the playing. Dial access types of tape deck consoles with outlets for individual or group use offer less freedom of control to the listener but are workable. For the music schools, stereo reception equipment with speakers capable of gaining high fidelity is essential. There is a need for small rooms and large rooms for group listening. Access to a piano keyboard is needed in the room.

3. For teaching, a seminar containing players for records and tapes is needed. Also, telephone connections to the central tape deck console is necessary so that records and tapes can be put on the console and heard in the seminar. If possible, the instructor should be able to control the progress of the playing. A piano in the room is desirable.

4. All listening stations should provide large enough table surface — at least two-by-four feet — so that listeners can read music scores while listening and also take notes.

5. As of 1972, it would appear that the development of cassettes and individual players would minimize the need for a dial access-multiple tape deck console system. Advantages lie not only in the cost factors but also in giving each listener the freedom to control the progress of the tape. The tapes are kept either on open shelves or charged out from a closed access desk.

A. BUSINESS ADMINISTRATION LIBRARIES

Only those types of departmental libraries having unique architectural problems are included. Business administration libraries share the problems one would find in social science libraries. The University of Colorado Business Administration Library is included in some detail because it is the most complete of any in the United States.

Colorado, University of Colorado, Business Library. Entrance view. Lobby separated by glass partition. Charging desk on left, library beyond.

Colorado, University of Colorado, Business Library. Card catalog in center. Current periodicals on left. Notice that low card catalog forces readers to sit down — not good.

Colorado, University
of Colorado, Business Li-
brary. Librarian in office in
front can see users of card
catalog and references.

Colorado, University
of Colorado, Business Li-
brary. Librarian's office as
seen from reading room. She
is invitingly available.

Colorado, University
of Colorado, Business Li-
brary. Bookstacks in center
of library. Reader stations
(three kinds) along outer
wall.

Colorado, University
of Colorado, Business Li-
brary. Carrels with dial
access to taped programs.

Colorado, University of Colorado, Business Library. Lounge chairs for current journals and newspapers.

Colorado, University of Colorado, Business Library. Corporation annual reports in separate room.

Colorado, University of Colorado, Business Library. Video tape recorder in carrel.

Colorado, University of Colorado, Business Library. High walled carrels.

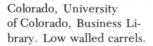

Colorado, University
of Colorado, Business Library. Low walled carrels.

Colorado, University
of Colorado, Business Library. More carrels.

Colorado, University
of Colorado, Business Library. A third type of carrel.

Colorado, University
of Colorado, Business Library. Photocopy machine
near current journals.

Colorado, University of Colorado, Business Library. Displays on front face of bookstacks.

Colorado, University of Colorado, Business Library. Microfilm reels on carousel.

Minnesota, University of Minnesota. Small reference section in central library building for Business Administration library.

Oregon, Portland State College. Business administration reference division in central library building.

Pennsylvania, University of Pennsylvania, Wharton School. Card catalog and reference center.

Utah, University of Utah. Current periodicals at back of room. Reference books on right. Charging desk and librarian's office behind camera. Few books but lots of reading tables.

B.   EDUCATION LIBRARIES

Education libraries have one unique facility: a curricular laboratory, which contains a variety of things: sample text books, courses of study, audiovisual materials, various kinds of electronic learning hardware, teaching graphics, etc.

California, University of California at Santa Barbara. Curriculum laboratory materials. Limited to printed materials.

New York, State University of New York at Albany. The ERIC reports in microfiche form are kept in drawers and are read in machines between cabinets.

Ohio, Bowling Green University. Curriculum laboratory materials. Contains much audiovisual material as well as printed materials.

Pennsylvania, Lafayette College. Curriculum laboratory. Courses of study in foreground. Texts in rear.

C. LAW LIBRARIES

Usually seat 90 percent of enrollment. The Southern Methodist University Law Library building, not completed in time for inclusion, will contain the best elements found in other college libraries. It should be one of the best.

California, University
of California at Los Angeles,
Law Library. One of the
few that keeps circulation
desk noise out of reading
room. Entrance to reading
room on right.

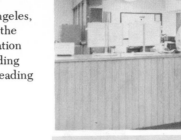

California, University
of California at Los Angeles.
One of few law libraries
that has carrels in reading
room — a group study
room.

California, University
of California at Los Angeles.
Entrance, with charging
desk beyond partition.
Much visual distraction in
this library and little
privacy. Has one group
study room.

England, Oxford Univer-
sity, Law Library. One
good way of making certain
that only able-bodied students will apply!

England, Oxford University, Law Library. Breaks with traditional architecture, but then Oxford has done this for centuries!

Florida, University of Florida, Law Library. Except for control problems caused by multiple entrances, this law library has used all the new ideas now commonly found in universities. Entrance and reserve desk outside reading room. See also pictures in Books and Readers section.

Georgia University of Georgia. Traditional law library with mezzanine. It cannot be expanded.

410

Georgia, University of Georgia, Law Library. Special carrels in separate room for honors students — but carrels are too small, students avoid them.

Illinois, University of Illinois, Law Library. Traditional law library *par excellence*. Charging desk in room. A goldfish bowl arrangement.

Illinois, University of Illinois, Law Library. Another view of the same.

Pennsylvania, Temple University. Single room with books along sides.

Tennessee, Vanderbilt University, Law Library. The familiar goldfish bowl and mezzanine.

Tennessee, Vanderbilt University, Law Library. Books on two sides. Tables in center.

Texas, University of Houston, Law Library. Has underground library with central atrium. Underground locations seem to create expansion problems. See University of Oregon Science Library.

Texas, University of
Houston, Law Library. Card
catalog and reference tools
on this side of atrium. Circulation desk and librarian's
office opposite front door.
Book collections beyond
atrium.

Texas, University of
Houston, Law Library. On
floor below, a series of
rooms, each filled with
carrels.

Texas, University of
Houston, Law Library.
Carrels with lockers.

Texas, University of Houston, Law Library. Looking towards center of library, where offices and charging desk are located.

Texas, University of Houston, Law Library. One of several group study rooms. Good.

Utah, University of Utah. All the traditional elements — mezzanine, goldfish bowl, circulation desk in reading room.

D. MEDICAL LIBRARIES — INCLUDING DENTISTRY AND NURSING

Very much like other science libraries except that medical students put great emphasis on reading the current journals immediately upon their arrival.

Massachusetts, Harvard University, Countway Medical Library. (See photographs in other sections.) Card catalog and current journals clearly visible from entrance.

Massachusetts, Harvard University, Countway Medical Library. Comfortable furniture for reading current journals. This type of current issue cabinet presents difficulties in keeping the journals visible and in place.

Massachusetts, Harvard University, Countway Medical Library. A group study room.

Massachusetts, Harvard University, Countway Medical Library. Small research studies appended to inner wall of atrium. Nice architectural trick but not very practical.

Michigan, Wayne State University, Medical Library. Reference collection.

Michigan, Wayne State University. Card catalog and reference collection. Telephone at end of card catalog for within-building communication.

Pennsylvania, University of Pennsylvania. Display of "this week's" issues of medical journals. Note tall exhibit book trucks.

Pennsylvania, University of Pennsylvania. New journals and reference area in background.

Pennsylvania, University
of Pennsylvania. Adminis-
tration office and reference
area to left.

Pennsylvania, University
of Pennsylvania. Exhibit
trucks.

Pennsylvania, University
of Pennsylvania. Split level
stacks. Not good. Elevators
are available but not close to
stairway.

Tennessee, Vanderbilt University, Medical Library.
Has nice series of alcoves for
current medical journals —
very good.

Wisconsin, University of Wisconsin at Madison, Medical Library. Good system for current serials records. File faces librarian here but rotates for public. See below.

Wisconsin, University of Wisconsin at Madison, Medical Library. Here file is available to public.

Wisconsin, University of Wisconsin at Madison, Medical Library. Convenient reference desk.

Wisconsin, University of Wisconsin at Madison, Medical Library. Good medical abstract and index shelves.

Wisconsin, University
of Wisconsin at Madison,
Medical Library. Nice place
for current journals and
books.

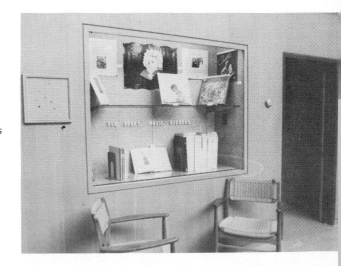

Wisconsin, University
of Wisconsin at Madison,
Medical Library. A wide
variety of reader station
facilities. Nicely arranged.

E. Music Libraries

There are no thoroughly satisfactory music libraries in any college
or university. The Universities of California at Berkeley and Santa
Barbara come closest, especially Santa Barbara.

California, University
of California at Berkeley,
Music Library. Entrance has
exhibit case.

California, University of California at Berkeley, Music Library. To right of entrance is room with individual tape and record players. No dial access.

California, University of California at Berkeley, Music Library. Beyond record player room is main reading room, with current periodicals in rear, bookstacks on left side.

California, University of California at Berkeley, Music Library. Current periodicals at rear of reading room and bookstacks at left.

California, University of California at Santa Barbara. Behind charging desk are record and tape players with outlets in seminars and individual listening rooms.

California, University of California at Santa Barbara. Beyond desk: lounge furniture, current periodicals, reference collection, and finally books.

California, University of California at Santa Barbara. Individual listening room has telephone connection to central control panel. There are several of these for listeners who need high fidelity equipment.

California, University of California at Santa Barbara. Seminar rooms have all kinds of playing equipment, including connection to central control panel.

California, University
of California at Santa
Barbara. Magnocord tape
reproducer Model 1024 to
make tapes from disks.
Feeds into main console.

F.   SCIENCE LIBRARIES

The University of Georgia Science Library building is the most successful science library building in the United States. Pictures of this library are included in various sections of this book and are not repeated here. Reference to them can be found in the Index.

Arizona, University of Arizona, Science Library. Three-to-four-level building. Each science department occupies one end of a floor. Main floor has central reference, circulation, and catalog services. Approximately 70,000 square feet.

California, University
of California at Berkeley,
Chemistry Library. Elegant
example of traditional single
departmental library.

California, University of California at Berkeley, Chemistry Library. Abstracts and reference books in Chemistry Library.

Connecticut, Yale University, Engineering Library. Entrance is at far end.

Connecticut, Yale University, Engineering Library. Reading room from entrance end. Books above and below mezzanine.

Connecticut, Yale University, Engineering Library. Well lighted study carrel.

Connecticut, Yale University, Engineering Library. Carrels and stacks on the mezzanine.

Connecticut, Yale University, Engineering Library. Current journals.

Connecticut, Yale University, Science Library. (90,000 square feet.) In basement of biology building.

Connecticut, Yale University, Science Library. Entrance to left, card catalog, photocopier, with reference desk on right. Book collection beyond columns.

Connecticut, Yale University, Science Library. Reading room with reference books on right. Bookstacks beyond reference books.

Connecticut, Yale University, Science Library. Biological abstracts in microfilm cassettes.

Connecticut, Yale University, Science Library. Computer console for consulting off-campus data banks.

Connecticut, Yale University, Science Library. Current journals in stacks.

Connecticut, Yale University, Science Library. Entrance to stacks on right side of reading room.

Oregon, University of Oregon, Science Library. Science abstracting and indexing services. Books and journals behind.

Oregon, University of Oregon, Science Library. Index tools for geology. Current periodicals are on opposite end of tables.

Oregon, University of Oregon. Underground science library next to science center. Central atrium.

Oregon, University
of Oregon, Science Library.
Current journals.

Oregon, University
of Oregon, Science Library.
Research carrels.

The New Architecture, Tufts University

VIII

The Building—
Structure and Details

A.   STRUCTURE

1. Modular Planning versus Fixed Function

In the older, fixed-function buildings each area — reading room, bookstacks, reference room, technical processes room, etc. — was designed specifically to house one function and there was little ability to transfer functions. In the so-called modular buildings — made up of cubes of space, each of which is capable of housing most library functions — the capacity for interchange is great. Almost all academic library buildings constructed since World War II are of this type.

The easiest way to understand these modular buildings is to look at the various floor layouts in Chapter V and to examine one or two cross sections.

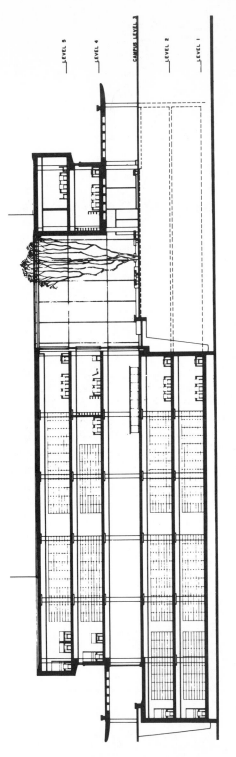

Missouri, Washington University. Cross section of building. Atrium placed near front of building to provide outside fenestration to reading rooms, and also as design element.

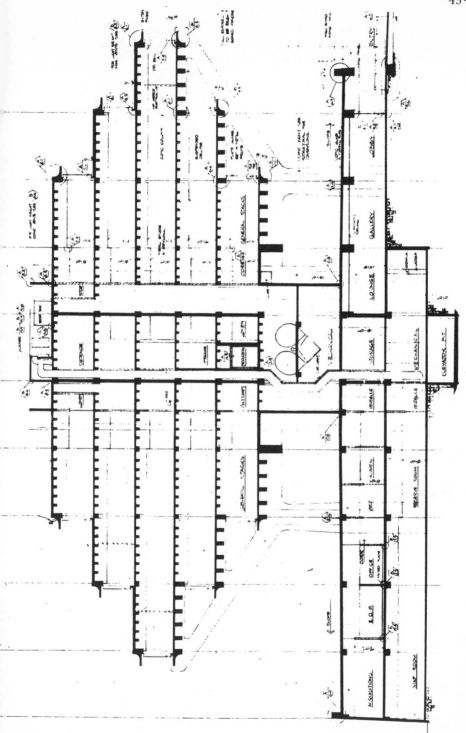

California, University of California at San Diego. Both below and above-ground sections are modular.

431

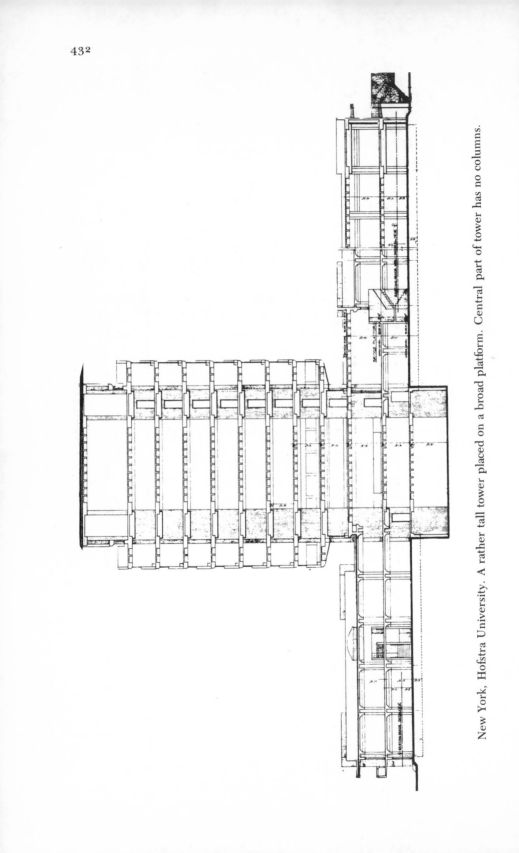

New York, Hofstra University. A rather tall tower placed on a broad platform. Central part of tower has no columns.

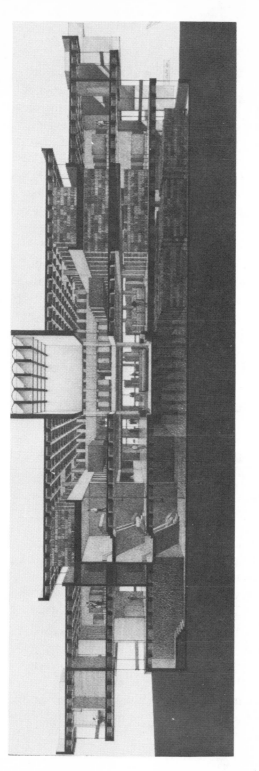

Rhode Island, Providence College. Although not all modules are same size, most of building is modular in nature.

2. *Provisions for Expansion*

Although there are several ways of slowing down the growth of book collections in a college or university (decentralizing the collection into other buildings on campus, using electronic communication technology, using compact storage systems, and reducing books to microforms), it would appear at the present time that none of these possibilities justifies the planning of a library building that is not capable of extensive enlargement. Specific provisions for enlargement are usually made at the time the original plans are drawn, even though the nature of future expansion units may change.

Even though modular planning eliminates or minimizes the difficulties that exist in expanding a fixed-function building, unless the site conditions are favorable and the non-movable core elements are placed properly, a modular building can present difficulties. The essential issues the architect keeps in mind are:

a. To plan the layout of the elements in the first unit so that when it is expanded the scheme of book and reader facilities will not be interrupted by structural elements that confuse the reader as he goes from the old to the new part.

Examples of the difficulties usually encountered in expanding a fixed-function building can be found at the Universities of Michigan, Illinois, Duke, and Washington.

Examples of proper expansion planning can be seen in the modular libraries at the Universities of Oregon, Iowa, and Northern Iowa.

b. To keep traffic lanes for the public and staff direct and easily followed.

c. To plan service facilities such as heating, air conditioning, and vertical transportation units so that they will be adequate to service the enlarged building, or so that additional facilities in the expanded unit will balance the facilities in the original structure.

d. To use knock-out materials in the exterior walls where expansion is to occur so that "sentimental" objections will not be raised where the addition is constructed.

e. To place towers, if they are used, on the edge of platforms rather than in their center, so that the towers can be enlarged.

f. To have clear concept of ultimate size of buildings so that plans can be made for the time when the building cannot be enlarged further.

g. To make certain that the site is suitable for the expansion program and that the site is earmarked for this purpose.

California, University of California at Berkeley, Undergraduate Library. Shaded area, used for classrooms with separate entrance, will be taken over by library as needed.

California, University of California at Los Angeles, Research Library. The first of two expansions. Modules added to one side for first expansion.

California, University of California at Santa Barbara. Tower can be doubled in size along back of long dimension.

California, University of California at Santa Cruz. Can be expanded at rear of building and by occupying non-library departments at opposite end of bridge from library.

California, Occidental College. Addition connected to old building with corridor. Roof line used as harmonizing element. Photo by Joe Friezer, News-Publicity Photographer, Los Angeles, California

Canada, Waterloo Lutheran University. Two levels being added to present building.

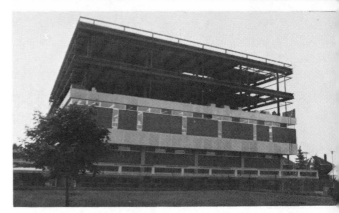

England, Birmingham Univeristy. Addition being placed as wing of original building.

England, Warwick University. Part of existing building used for non-library function until needed — bookstore and departmental rooms.

Georgia, Georgia Institute of Technology. Large addition placed at end of original building. Additional levels can be added later.

Illinois, University of Illinois. Fifth stack addition under construction. No attempt to match original building.

Indiana, Notre Dame University. Alternate ranges of bookshelves. Can be expanded later.

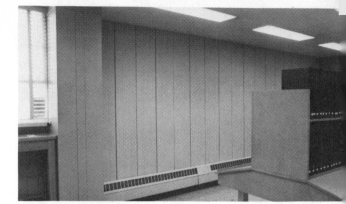

Iowa, University of Iowa. Easily removed metal panel walls were used where expansion was to take place.

Michigan, University of Michigan. Large addition placed at rear of original building. No possibility of matching original style.

Michigan, Wayne University, Medical Library. Note knockout back wall for expansion.

Nevada, University of Nevada. Areas can be filled in under arches at end, also at back of building.

New York, Rochester University. Expanding this fixed function tower library was difficult. Addition works well but some articulation problems are not completely satisfactory.

North Carolina, Duke University. Link between old and new.

North Carolina, Duke University. Junction point between old and new — inside.

North Carolina, Duke University. Addition matched strong Gothic structure.

Oregon, University of Oregon. Junction point between first and second addition — impossible to distinguish old from new.

Oregon, Reed College. Addition placed at rear of building architecturally of high quality.

Pennsylvania, Beaver College. Pre-cast slabs can be removed and addition placed on this side.

Rhode Island, Brown University. Can add two to four shelves at top of existing ranges. Will have to use ladders to reach books.

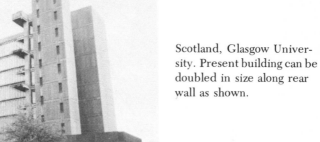

Scotland, Glasgow University. Present building can be doubled in size along rear wall as shown.

Scotland, Glasgow University. No doubt that this wall was meant for expansion. Good!

South Carolina, Clemson University. Left large areas in basement for expansion. Building can be expanded vertically also, two more levels.

Tennessee, Vanderbilt University. Reasonably successful expansion of fixed function building.

Tennessee, Vanderbilt University. The junction point between new and old on each level.

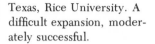

Texas, Rice University. A difficult expansion, moderately successful.

Texas, Southwestern University. Junction area used for current periodicals. Courtyard on left.

Texas, University of Texas at El Paso. Without doubt the most attractive addition in United States. Addition in front, with courtyard, was too small (Texas formulas!) Photo by Darst-Ireland Photograph, El Paso, Texas.

Texas, University of Texas at El Paso. Stair tower from courtyard. Photo by Darst-Ireland Photograph, El Paso, Texas.

Texas, University of Texas at El Paso. From new addition go up this stairway into old building through courtyard. Photo by Darst-Ireland Photograph, El Paso, Texas.

Utah, University of Utah. First expansion will be to move walls under overhang to outside edge. Further expansion is impossible.

Washington, Washington State University. Side of library facing parking lot can be removed and a large addition made in parking lot.

3. Enlarging versus Building a New Building

The problem of deciding whether buildings should be remodeled, enlarged or abandoned in favor of a new structure is always an individual decision because buildings are all different from each other, site problems are never the same, and campus regulations are always unique.

The process of deciding involves two questions, the first of which should be answered in the affirmative before the second is tackled.

The first question is whether the original building and the addition together will result in a satisfactory, properly functioning building, as determined by the criteria generally accepted by the library building experts.

If the answer, by a consensus of experts, is no, the question of costs is irrelevant. If it is yes, then the second question is whether the cost is more or less than the cost of a new building. If the cost is considerably less, the institution probably goes ahead. But if it is the same as, or more than, the cost of a new building and if a proper site is available, the institution would normally go for a new building.

There are cases where the institution has to choose the remodeling and enlarging method even though the results will not be too good and the cost is high because of site and money considerations. Both the University of Michigan and the University of California at Berkeley are examples of this kind of decision.

Fixed-function buildings seldom enlarge satisfactorily unless a division of labor between them and their addition can be made. At Oregon, for example, the original building was used primarily for a library school; at Northwestern for special collections; at Colorado for a college or undergraduate library. At UCLA, Emory, and Cornell new structures were built but the original building was converted into an undergraduate library.

The newer modular buildings almost always can be enlarged easily (two exceptions being Hardin Simmons in Texas and San Fernando State College in California). Examples are: the University of Iowa, University of Northern Iowa, Wayne University, the University of Georgia, the University of Idaho, and Washington State University.

B.   THE STRUCTURE — PHYSICAL DETAILS

1. Fenestration and Ventilation

Fenestration. Lighting technology is sufficiently advanced to permit the planning of windowless buildings if such are needed.

Since the use of natural lighting is confined to an area up to six feet from the windows, functions should be placed there that fit this kind of space and that do not destroy the psychological value of being able to look out and see a fine view or the state of the weather. This means reader stations — not book shelving.

The use of glass walls has created heating and ventilation problems that are difficult or costly to solve. Tinted and heat-absorbing glass distort the view. Draperies, venetian blinds, etc. shut out the view as well as the glare. Heat screens obstruct the view. The use of metal perforated walls, as at Oregon State University and the New Orleans Public Library, do solve the problems of heat and glare but they obstruct the view and hence have to be justified on the basis of design. The use of exterior panels, baffles, and overhangs to solve the problem of glare and excessive heat and cold are at best an expensive, superficial solution about as logical as rubbing lineament on an arthritic joint.

The current architectural habit of using functional fenestration on all levels of the library except the street level, which is enclosed with window walls, and then restricting the size of the main floor, with the upper floors serving as an overhang to keep the sun out, is illogical because it lessens the amount of floor space available on the main floor, which needs to be the largest, not the smallest, level in the library.

Ventilation. Appropriate filtering systems are provided to keep out gases that damage books and dirt that annoys people and injures paper. The nature of the system used will depend on the kinds, if any, of gases in the air.

Temperature ranges from seventy to seventy-two degrees are ideal but are difficult to achieve because there are so many different kinds of spaces in the library and because of the cost. Stuffy air seems to bother readers more than temperatures beyond the above ranges. At least eight turnovers of air per hour should be provided where people work.

Humidity levels for maximum protection to books should be kept above forty-five and below fifty-five degrees.

Local temperature controls in special rooms such as faculty research studies, seminars, and staff offices are desirable but expensive.

Ventilation systems that are beyond the competence of the typical campus maintenance staffs seldom produce satisfactory results.

2. Lighting

People differ widely in their opinions of what constitutes good lighting or the kinds of fixtures, light qualities and levels necessary to achieve it. (See K. D. Metcalf, *Library Lighting*, Association of Research Libraries, Washington, D.C., 1970.)

Many types of light fixtures and layouts are in use that produce results acceptable to library readers. In fact, one might observe that readers seem not to be much aware of lighting qualities unless they are so bad that they cannot see at all. Other things, such as type of reader stations, their locations, seem to be more important than lighting.

Recessed bullet light fixtures have been extensively used by architects, although it is difficult to see why because these fixtures produce poor lighting except in the area directly below them; and they are expensive to maintain.

The best general reading room results seem to have been achieved when the architect has used a wide type of fixture with a plastic lens between the fluorescent bulbs and the reader.

Most architects use fixtures easily available on the market; a few have designed their own.

There are many installations that cause excessive glare either through the use of exposed bulbs or improper cove installations.

Widespread use of carrels with wings on three sides of the readers creates special lighting problems, especially if the carrels contain a shelf, i.e. the problem of shadows on the reading surface. Light fixtures attached to the bottom of the shelf solve the problem, but these create the necessity of fixing the carrels to one place because of the need for electrical outlets.

In bookstacks, one finds light fixtures running parallel to the bookstacks and at right angles to them. In all instances the ceilings have been high enough to permit lowering the lens to replace bulbs.

It is known that light rays cause deterioration of books directly and indirectly. (See Feller, R.L., "The Deteriorating Effects of Light on Museum Objects," *Museum News*, vol. 42, June, 1964. Technical Supplement, pp. VI–VIII.) Light rays themselves cause deterioration and heat, resulting from light, also causes deterioration. It is best to use a glass or plastic lens between fluorescent bulbs and books and to see that light fixtures do not raise temperatures in bookstack areas.

FENESTRATION

Arizona, Arizona State University. The Arizona sun is kept out by slit windows on second level. Overhang on first level causes glare problems.

California, California Institute of Technology. Formalized windows OK on north side but give too much light on other side of building.

Canada, Guelph University. Slit windows at eye level on each floor. Good results.

Colorado, Loretta Heights College. The dilemma — mountains on west are great view but sun causes glare — pull draperies and you can't see the mountains. OK in mornings and when moon is full.

England, East Anglia University. New universities go in for larger windows with vertical venetian blinds.

England, Essex University. Fine view of campus lake out of these windows.

France, Nice University, Letters Library. Clerestory windows as well as in walls of glass.

France, Nice University, Letters Library. Exterior view of clerestory system on roof.

Germany, Giessen University. Special framed windows.

Illinois, University of Chicago. Faculty study rooms in the pods — good fenestration.

Illinois, Northwestern University. Extensive use of slit windows. Good fenestration throughout building.

Iowa, University of Northern Iowa. Slit windows with one exception for "framed view" on each wall. A good system.

Louisiana, Tulane University. Glass walls on main level under slight overhang.

Massachusetts, Amherst College. Slit windows at eye level. A functional design.

Massachusetts, Clark University. Dramatic use of windows is interesting. Much glare.

Massachusetts, Clark University. Two types. At top, small windows are for study rooms. Boxes are for view.

Massachusetts, Clark University. Sloping windows. See earlier picture for interior results.

Michigan, Wayne University, Medical Library. Combination of slit windows at eye level and horizontal strips above. Good. Similar to Amherst.

Michigan, Wayne University, Medical Library. Close-up of windows.

New York, State University of New York at Albany. Uses "framed view" idea with great restraint in other parts of building.

New York, Wells College. Windows of this type create glare problems and what is there to see anyway?

Ohio, Bowling Green University. Slit windows for research studies.

Oregon, Oregon State University. Metal screens used on three sides. Light comes in but view is obstructed.

Oregon, Oregon State University. Close-up of screen.

Oregon, Oregon State University. Glass wall on north side.

Pennsylvania, Bryn Mawr College. Small windows, similar to Northwestern.

456

Rhode Island, Brown University. Slit windows give researchers a chance to see what weather is doing without creating glare.

Scotland, Glasgow University. Plastic wall. One cannot see anything. Recessed barrel light fixtures obviously do not supply enough light — see shadows on floor.

South Carolina, Clemson University. On north side a glass wall gives good campus view in front atrium.

South Dakota, University of South Dakota. The ideal combination — slit windows for work, and see next photograph.

South Dakota, University
of South Dakota. Big win-
dows for "framed view" in
lounge area.

Texas, Abilene Christian
College. Tall slit windows.
Good results.

Texas, North Texas State
University. Few windows
and those are small.

Texas, Rice University.
Good fenestration for re-
search studies.

Utah, University of Utah.
Slit windows except on recessed main floor.

Washington, Pacific
Lutheran University. Used
"framed view" to good
advantage.

Washington, D.C., George-town University. Serrated wall. Solves problems of glare on sunny side.

Wisconsin, University of Wisconsin at Madison, Medical Library. Overhang keeps some sunlight out of large basement windows.

LIGHTING

Canada, Guelph University. Indirect lighting around columns. Strip fluorescent fixtures elsewhere. The column lighting is more for design than function.

England, Essex University. Fixtures can be run in either direction. The ceiling pan is four and a half feet square.

Idaho, University of Idaho. Egg crate lens below long strip fixtures.

Indiana, Indiana University, Research Library. Large plastic covered fixture. Air supply and exhaust on edges of fixture.

Iowa, Luther College. Square fixture recessed in each ceiling bay. Air supply and exhaust on edge of bays. Excellent lighting.

Kansas, Fort Hays State College. Ventilation inlets on edges of fixtures. Ceiling in rear has been dropped about eighteen inches.

Louisiana, Tulane University. Drop lights in lobby. Armstrong fixture in rear. Results are obvious.

Massachusetts, Harvard University, Radcliffe College. Combination of indirect lighting and direct lighting from fixture in each bay. Custom designed fixture.

Michigan, Wayne University, Medical Library. Plastic lens at bottom of bays where needed. More can be installed if needed.

Nebraska, University of Nebraska, Agriculture Library. Louverall type of plastic lens below each fixture. On edge drop lights are supposed to light carrels but do not. Egg crate fixture below the plastic lens.

New York, Rochester University. Asia Room. Drop lights here cause glare. Not a good system.

New York, State University of New York at Albany. Light fixtures splay out from columns consistently throughout building. Good general lighting but creates problems in small rooms.

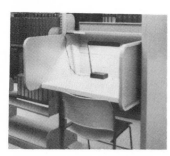

New York, Wells College. Desk lamp in carrels.

New York, Wells College. Drop lights in ceiling.

New York, Wells College. Drop lights and splayed arrangement in hexagon stacks area. Drop lights in front of stacks. Not a system to be copied.

New Zealand, Auckland University. Extensive use of clerestory indirect lighting and fluorescent fixtures. Shadows under shelves.

North Carolina, Duke
University. Combination of
different shaped fixtures.
Drop lights over circula-
tion desk records on right.

Oregon, Portland State College. Has square fixture in
each bay.

Pennsylvania, Bryn Mawr
College. Drop lights in
lobby and indirect lighting
over card catalog. Latter
causes glare, former does
not give enough light.

Pennsylvania, Bryn Mawr
College. Windows do not
give enough light for carrels.

465

Pennsylvania, Temple University. Ceiling fixture baffles seem out of place in a library.

Sweden, Chalmers Technical University. Ceiling fixtures plus table lights.

Sweden, Chalmers Technical University. Good ceiling bay type of lighting in reference room.

Sweden, Chalmers Technical University. Side view of ceiling fixture.

Texas, Northern Texas University, Denton. Large fixture with plastic lens. Ventilation through slits on edge of fixture.

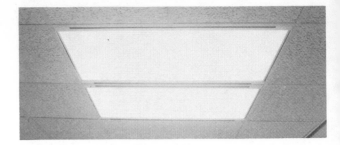

Lighting — Bookstacks

California, University of California at Los Angeles. Lights at right angle to stacks. Two fixtures for a twelve-foot range.

California, University of California at Santa Cruz. Fixtures run both ways. Co-ordinated with aisle widths.

Florida, University of Jacksonville. Fixtures run at right angles to ranges — three fixtures for an eighteen-foot range.

Georgia, Emory University. Lights attached to stack ranges. A rather permanent installation.

Louisiana, Tulane University. These fixtures give almost same results as louverall type — manufactured by Armstrong.

Massachusetts, Harvard University, Countway Medical Library. Fixtures run at right angles to ranges.

Ohio, Bowling Green State University. Right angle to ranges.

Pennsylvania, University of Pennsylvania. Parallel to ranges. Bare fluorescent tubes used.

LIGHTING — CARRELS

Kansas, St. Benedict's College. Carrels with shelves need supplemental lighting under the shelf.

Maryland, Johns Hopkins University. Shelf lighting with quite good overhead lights.

Pennsylvania, Lafayette College. Recessed barrel fixtures in ceiling. Lights under shelf in carrels.

Pennsylvania, Lafayette
College. Another view of
same.

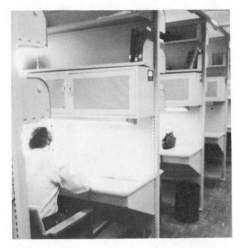

Texas, Rice University.
Carrels in stacks — well
lighted. Locked boxes
above.

Wisconsin, Beloit College.
Light placed on wall beside
carrels. Good lighting.

3. Carpeting

Carpeting is used now in most libraries in most parts of the library, not as an economy measure but to help establish the kind of environment a library should have and to control the noise levels.

England, Birmingham University, Addition. Much use is made abroad of Heugafeld carpeting (in eighteen-inch squares). It does not have to be cemented and can be changed to replace worn spots.

England, Birmingham University. One square removed to show ease of installation.

Massachusetts, Tufts University. How students use carpeting!

Michigan, Grand Valley State College. The feeling one wants in a library.

4. Cloak Rooms

Few libraries try to maintain cloak rooms in which readers are required to leave their coats because they cannot afford to staff these rooms adequately. Most have tried to provide facilities near where students work so that students may take care of their own clothing. A few examples are included.

Canada, University of Waterloo. Provides coat room on each floor visible to some of the reader stations.

Iowa, Luther College. Neat arrangement along reading room walls.

Iowa, University of Northern Iowa. Uses rod at end of stack ranges. This is the most commonly used method.

5. Paraplegics — Provisions for

Federal regulations now require libraries to provide ramps, hardware, elevators, and toilets that can be operated by paraplegics and places for wheelchairs in reading rooms. A few examples (with name of institution omitted) of typical mistakes are included.

Beautiful but not sensible.

A back entrance but ramp is too steep.

Split level stacks. Yes, there is an elevator at other end of room.

6. Exhibitions — Facilities

Arizona, Arizona State University. Exhibit case in front atrium.

Colorado, University of Colorado, Business Administration Library. Display racks with various kinds of facilities.

Delaware, University of Delaware. Attractive exhibit cases in front lobby.

England, East Anglia University. Special panels on main floor for hanging pictures and other exhibits.

Kansas, Mt. St. Scholastica College. Uses wall for pictures and hanging shelves. Very nice.

Massachusetts, Harvard University, Radcliffe College. Art gallery.

Michigan, Grand Valley State College. Tall exhibit case used to divide an area.

Michigan, University
of Michigan, Undergraduate
Library. An art gallery for
instructional purposes.

Michigan, University
of Michigan, Undergraduate
Library. Same.

Minnesota, University
of Minnesota. Cases in rare
book room.

Missouri, University of
Missouri at Rolla. Large
panel in front lobby.

Missouri, Stephens College. Wall used for shelves, pictures.

Missouri, Washington University. Wall exhibit used as room divider.

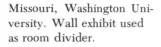

New York, Cornell University. Rare book room cases in lobby.

Oregon, Oregon State University. Wall exhibit as room divider.

Oregon, Pacific Lutheran University. Exhibit case in stack area.

Pennsylvania, Drexel Institute of Technology. Column cover for new book jackets.

Pennsylvania, Kutztown State College. Cases in Education Library house gift collection.

Pennsylvania, Lafayette College. Displays on wall panels and in cases.

Pennsylvania, Lehigh University, Science Library. Students protest pollution by exibiting collected junk.

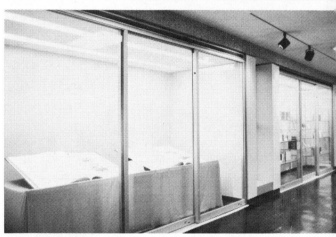

Pennsylvania, University of Pennsylvania, Wharton School. Cases in entrance lobby between two parts of library complex.

Wisconsin, Beloit College. Built-in exhibit case near entrance.

Tennessee, Belmont College. An art room at end of main reading room.

7. Screens to Divide Rooms

Idaho, University of Idaho. Long room divided into thirds. Frame with round wooden rods.

Michigan, Michigan Technological University. Screen made of bricks.

Oklahoma, University of Oklahoma. Semi-partition walls divide room into thirds.

Washington, Pacific Lutheran University. A browsing corner separated by screen.

8. *Stairways*

California, University
of California at Santa Cruz.
At end of building. This
unobtrusive circular stairway is properly designed:
you face narrow part of
step as you ascend, wide
part as you descend.

England, Kent University.
Puts stairwell outside the
structure.

England, York University.
A central feature of the
building. Placed at one end
of central atrium.

France, University of Marseille, Letters Library. France tends to put its main stairways in middle of central atrium.

Indiana, Earlham College. A modest stairway on back side of library, opposite entrance.

Iowa, University of Northern Iowa. Second floor view of main stairwell.

Massachusetts, Amherst College. Modest stairway in front of entrance. Reference desk is under stair landing.

Massachusetts, Harvard University, Countway Medical Library. Elegant oval stairwell in middle of building.

Pennsylvania, Bryn Mawr College. Massive — in end atrium.

Ohio, Wooster College. Main stairway to right of front door. Convenient, if legal.

Tennessee, Fiske University. An attractive central stairwell. Well placed.

Tennessee, Scarritt College. Graceful and properly located.

Washington, Pacific Lutheran University. In middle of atrium toward rear of building.

9. Food Services

One of the small but stubborn problems in American libraries is that of providing facilities for students to get a snack and a drink of coffee, or other beverages. The usual solution is to place automatic dispensers in a corridor, with no pleasant place to sit. This invites abuse and usually gets it.

A few libraries have tried to solve the problem by providing appropriate facilities.

England, Warwick University. Café in library. Very pleasant.

England, York University. A nice café. Fairly large.

Georgia, Emory University. A place for café and coffee bar to be installed later. Located on street level entrance.

Indiana, Indiana University. Large cafeteria for staff, students and faculty. University of Colorado has small coffee bar in honors section, University of Michigan has one in undergraduate library. Radcliffe has nice one on top floor.

Sweden, Chalmers Technical University. Not large but nice.

Sweden, Chalmers Technical University. Entrance to café on second ("first") floor.

Catalog Carrels, University of Minnesota

IX

Special Staff Offices
and Workrooms in
Academic Libraries

A. STAFF OFFICES

THE size and requirements of library staff offices are not uniform, but vary among the various departments. Offices for heads of departments in technical processes divisions are located where the librarian can be visible to the faculty who need to discuss problems and also so that the head can oversee the staff of the department. Since technical processes decisions are usually arrived at by groups, these offices are usually large enough for small committees.

Reference staffs also need to be visible; and they need shelf or counter work space and lots of shelving. However, reference offices do not seat more than two or three people at a time and hence are not as large as technical processes offices.

Georgia, Emory University. Head of order department has glass-front office located near front of technical processes.

Idaho, University of Idaho.
Office for science librarian is
quite large because of work
room in rear.

Illinois, Northwestern University. Office for head of
catalog department located
at front of technical processes area.

Indiana, Indiana University.
Philosophy and history of
science subject specialist on
one of top floors of bookstacks. Room for one visitor
only.

Indiana, Indiana University.
Literature subject specialist
in bookstacks is larger area
because of large amount of
material Dr. Shipps handles.

Iowa, University of Northern Iowa. Head of cataloging
is located at front of
department.

Minnesota, University
of Minnesota. University
bibliographer, Jim Kingsley,
needs large office in center
of technical processes area.

North Carolina, Duke.
Office for head of cataloging
department at one end
of department.

Ohio, Ohio Northern Uni-
versity. Office for head of
cataloging department
located to one side of
cataloging department.

B.   Staff Lounges

Most college and university libraries provide a lounge room
where staff members can go on their "break" for rest, talk and
food. These differ from one another only in their location, size,
and kind of furniture. A few have a cot room for staff who are ill.

Georgia, Emory University.
Has facilities for lounging
and eating.

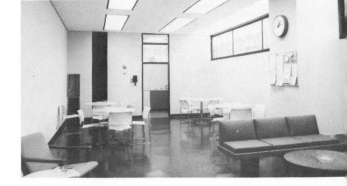

Illinois, Northwestern University. To be shared by staff and faculty. Kitchen on left.

Indiana, Indiana University. Since most of staff who use the room are in technical processes, room is located near technical processes.

Minnesota, University of Minnesota. Large room, mostly for eating. Building has plenty of lounge furniture in reading rooms.

Rhode Island, Brown University. A well appointed room.

Scotland, Glasgow University. One of the best staff lounges anywhere.

South Dakota, University of South Dakota. Staff room with cot room behind. Good arrangement. Combined refrigerator, hot plate and dish storage unit is typical.

Sweden, Chalmers Technical University. Staff lounge with the usual Swedish charm.

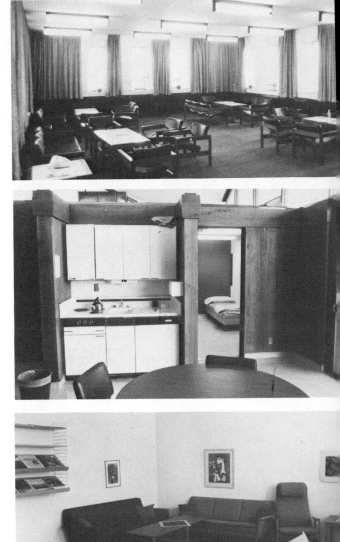

C.   Book Repair Rooms

Most libraries send their books out to library binderies for repair, but a few maintain a specialist to do book restoration and repair work on rare books. This is mostly hand work and does not require elaborate equipment or a great deal of space. The Storm Bindery in Sedona, Arizona, for example, is contained in a room not more than twenty-by-thirty feet.

Two pictures of the book repair room at Brown University are included to show the kind of equipment needed and the way such a room is arranged. The work done here is high quality hand work, not quantity production.

Rhode Island, Brown University. Some libraries do book preservation work on rare books. Here is some of equipment required.

Rhode Island, Brown University. Other end of room.

D.   Data Processing and Machine Rooms

During the last ten years libraries have introduced various types of machines for bookkeeping, for computerized circulation systems, for inter and intra library communication systems, and for consulting data banks. Some libraries have conducted extensive experiments on various phases of automation and each installation would appear to be unique. Common to all is the need for access to power and telephone wires, channels for TV, and computer cables. Some idea of the equipment involved is shown.

California, University
of California at Los Angeles.
Fairly typical data processing installation for punched
card record keeping. (UCLA
does much more than that
shown.)

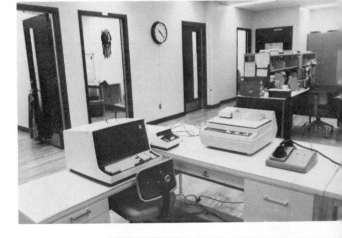

California, University
of California at San Diego.
Computer console with data
phone. Office for data processing staff in rear. Machine
is used to consult data banks.

Delaware, University
of Delaware. Many libraries
use teletype machines for
inter-library loans and other
communication.

Florida, University of Florida. Data processing room,
mostly for punched card
type of work.

Georgia, Georgia Institute of Technology. Data processing room about thirty-by-forty feet for various types of automation work.

Pennsylvania, Lehigh University. Various kinds of computer terminals and printout machines are shown in center for study of progressive learning.

Pennsylvania. Lehigh University, Science Library. Closer view showing some of cables involved.

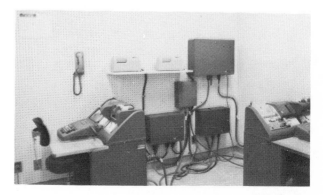

Advantages of Carpeting, Tufts University

X

The Human Part—
Plus and Minus

ALTHOUGH many good architectural solutions to library building problems — and some bad ones — have been presented in this report, a summary of some of the best mixed in with a few of the ridiculous would seem an appropriate summary of the text.

Arizona, Arizona State University. One of the truly beautiful buildings in the country. Moat brings light to basement level.

California, University
of California at Berkeley,
Undergraduate Library. An
outdoor reading court on
rear of building at basement
level. To be used for
chamber music concerts too.

California, University
of California at Los Angeles,
Research Library. Balcony
reading room overlooking
campus is nice, and func-
tional too.

California, University
of California at San Diego.
Shape of building enabled
architect to create some
spectacular views.

California, University of California at Santa Cruz. Central atrium is most appropriate for its setting and does not interfere with proper functioning of library.

California, University of California at Santa Cruz, Adlai Stevenson College Library. A small, intimate library. Atrociously lighted but room has nice feeling.

California, Chabot College. Round building creates new concept of space and is functional for this type of institution — community college. Both enrollment and book collection are limited.

California, Chabot College.
Bulletin board used for
cartoons, notices, etc.

Canada, University of
Waterloo. If you are going
to use a platform and tower,
this is the way to do it.

Canada, University of
Waterloo. An easy place to
rest in the stacks.

Connecticut, Yale University. Beinecke Library. You either love it or hate it. I think this part is great.

England, Essex University. Wordsworth would have written a poem about this view from reading room.

England, Lancaster University. Nice mural next to card catalog.

England, Warwick University. An architect's idea — sand-filled partition to kill sound transmission. The partition leaks!

England, York University. Charging desk in atrium lighted by a suspended cover. Also protects staff from falling objects.

Georgia, Georgia Institute of Technology. Architect deserves credit for not being afraid to change style of addition to meet GIT needs.

Germany, University of
Frankfurt. One of few
German university libraries
where you can approach
books directly, but not in
the stacks!

Holland, Delft Technological University. Interesting
way to house current issues
of periodicals where space is
limited.

Illinois, University of Chicago. Chicago's vistas are
not great but immediate
architectural environment
is nice to look at. "Framed
view" type of fenestration.
Very good.

Illinois, Illinois Wesleyan
University. Nice carrel with
privacy and slight view of
outside from window on left
of carrel.

Louisiana, Tulane University. Good group study room. Seats four, has blackboard and can be well supervised.

Massachusetts, Clark University. Massive columns take up immense amount of space, apparently to free central bookstack area of columns — not at all necessary.

Massachusetts, Tufts University. Sculptural display in roof-lighted semi-atrium.

Michigan, University
of Michigan, Central Li-
brary. "Visiting the iniquity
of the fathers upon the chil-
dren unto the third and
fourth generation . . ."
Exodus, XX,5

Minnesota, University
of Minnesota. Just a nice
place to study.

Missouri, Washington Uni-
versity. This courtyard is
great example of one way of
merging utility and beauty.

New Mexico, College of
Santa Fe. Excellent solution
to fenestration problem in
country where sun shines
brightly most of the time.

New York, Cornell Univer-
sity. Office work space for a
book-centered librarian.

New York, Cornell Univer-
sity, Undergraduate Li-
brary. Facing facts of life.

New York, Rochester University, Addition. Junction point between old and new. They live in harmony.

New York, State University of New York at Albany, Potted plants and lounge chairs create a nice place to read at ends of bookstacks.

New York, State University of New York at Albany. Not practical because of noise penetration on second floor but a beautiful lobby.

Ohio, John Carroll University. Pleasant view from entrance.

Oklahoma, Oklahoma State University. Grouping faculty research studies in isolated spot like this gives utmost privacy.

Pennsylvania, Haverford College. Placing mezzanine in church nave produced good results.

Scotland, Glasgow University. Harmonizes well with old surrounding buildings. Placing fixed core elements outside building frees center of building for library use.

Texas, Abilene Christian College. This is what a group study room is for.

514

Texas, Southern Methodist University, Science Library. It is plastic but result is good.

Utah, Brigham Young University. In the arid West this oasis between entrance and browsing room is Godsend.

Wisconsin, Beloit College. Architect created many nice views from reading rooms.

Glasgow University

XI

Conclusions About Planning

THIS study has shown that in recent years architects have developed a wide variety of solutions to most of the library building planning problems faced by colleges and universities. In terms of needed information and good examples to follow, there is no longer any reason why each new building cannot be perfect in its functioning. A few problems needing further attention will be mentioned at the end of this chapter.

As to aesthetics, too, there is a tremendous variety from the simplest unadorned square box to the lavishly sculptured free-form enclosures.

It is interesting to observe the evolution of the process by which architects began, after World War II, to work with the "modular" or loft type of planning and to embellish it with familiar architectural graces to conform to their concept, and to that of the general public, of the qualities an academic library building should have. There was a period at the end of World War II when university librarians (at least some of those in large universities in the Cooperative Committee on Library Building Plans) seemed to have the upper hand and were able to insist that their architects design buildings that met the necessary requirements.

And, as can be seen from this study, most of the architects have indeed designed buildings that meet the requirements of the present and the future, insofar as we know them, very well indeed.

But in recent years there has been some architectural backsliding and we now have some buildings that do not possess the functional qualities that are found in the typical modular library, especially in their lack of capacity for adaptability and expansion. This counter-trend, if it is really one, is of great concern to librarians who are aware of the deficiencies of the pre-modular library buildings and who are also aware of the advantages of the new. Their concern is not that some of the new buildings are too beautiful, but rather that their beauty is provided at the expense of the functional qualities an academic library should have, and that their cost is too high.

A strong case can be made for the charge that architectural forms that do not contribute to the functioning of a library could be called decadent architecture. This aspect of the problem will not be debated.

Library building costs, however, are of great concern. In view of the known book collection growth patterns facing colleges and universities as well as the developments in miniaturization, the increased use of non-print media, and the potential dispersal of some academic functions, it does seem that a college or university should first of all make certain that its library building is fully adaptable, and second, that it should not invest unnecessarily large sums in architectural qualities unrelated to function. Today does not appear to be a time when a library building should be created as an art object for the ages.

This situation is perhaps analogous to that of the parents of a young boy who outgrows his shoes every few months. Only the very rich or foolish would purchase the most expensive shoes unless they were known to be better for the boy's growing feet than less expensive shoes would be.

And, as this study shows, many of the library buildings that are best from the point of functioning are not the most costly.

In retrospect, I would choose the following buildings as being the most successful — not in rank order.

Colleges: Abilene Christian College, Amherst College, Luther College, Mt. St. Scholastica College.

Small universities or state colleges: Austin Peay State College, Ohio Northern University, Pacific Lutheran University, University of South Dakota.

Medium or large universities: University of Chicago, Indiana University, University of Minnesota, University of Northern Iowa.

Special Libraries: University of California at Berkeley, Undergraduate library; University of Georgia, Science Library; University of Oregon, Science Library; Southern Methodist University, Law Library.

British universities: East Anglia University, Edinburgh University, Glasgow University (recognizing its temporary entrance problem), Lancaster University.

Continental libraries: Chalmers Technological University (even though it was designed too small), Lumminy Library at the University of Nice; Nanterre University.

PROBLEMS THAT HAVE NOT YET BEEN SOLVED

Good architectural solutions in rich variety have now been provided for all the traditional physical plant problems academic libraries have faced. To be sure, there is no way of proving fully that one kind of facility or system is better than other kinds; but then there is no way of proving that one can participate in religious ceremonies better in the Coventry Cathedral in England than in the National Cathedral in Washington. One can, of course, ask people their preferences, but these really are not worth much because almost never does the individual have access to all kinds of facilities at the same time. His responses do not have much validity. And then, of course, the effect of environment is not always direct or recognizable at the conscious level.

The fact is that a planner of a new library can, from the information in the report, visit relevant libraries and decide for himself the things he likes.

But there are two areas where the physical facilities have not been properly thought out: provisions for the use of microforms and for so-called audiovisual materials.

Donald C. Holmes' study of the microform problem for A.R.L. should lead to the design of proper facilities for their use.

As for the audiovisual software and hardware, changes in both have come so fast that no one can make the problem stand still long enough for proper analysis. Each type of software will probably require a different kind of use station. Basic to all is the need for working surface to take notes, use typewriters, photocopy machines, sound recorders, etc. and to spread out books and related materials. To provide room for these things, the use stations will surely have to keep the hardware off the working table surface.

The location of use stations would logically be near the basic book collections so that all learning materials can be physically integrated.

Once these two types of problems are solved, and they are not basically architectural problems, there is no reason why each library building cannot be perfect — until a new batch of problems arises.

Appendix I
List of Libraries Included
— in this Study

Alabama	------
Alaska	------
Arizona	Arizona State University; University of Arizona, Science and Music; Cochise College; University of Northern Arizona; Prescott College
Arkansas	------
California	California Institute of Technology; University of California at Berkeley, Undergraduate, various departmental libraries; University of California at Los Angeles, General, Undergraduate and Law; University of California at San Diego, General and Undergraduate; University of California at Santa Barbara, General and Music; University of California at Santa Cruz (and Adlai Stevenson College Library); Cate School; Chabot College; Stanford University, Undergraduate; Westmont College
Colorado	Colorado College; Colorado State University; University of Colorado, Honors and Business; Loretta Heights College; Regis College; Southern Colorado College; Temple Buell College
Connecticut	Yale University, Beinecke, Art, Engineering, Science
Delaware	University of Delaware
Florida	Florida Southern College; Florida Technological University; University of Florida, General, Undergraduate and Law; University of Jacksonville; Miami University; University of Tampa
Georgia	Georgia Institute of Technology; University of Georgia, Law and Science; Emory University
Hawaii	------
Idaho	University of Idaho at Moscow

Illinois	University of Chicago; Illinois State University; University of Illinois, General, Undergraduate and Law; Illinois Wesleyan University; Northwestern University
Indiana	Earlham College; Indiana University; Notre Dame University
Iowa	University of Iowa; Luther College; University of Northern Iowa
Kansas	Fort Hays State College; University of Kansas, Medical; Mt. St. Scholastica College; St. Benedict's College
Kentucky	-----
Louisiana	Tulane University
Maine	-----
Maryland	Johns Hopkins University
Massachusetts	Amherst College; Boston University; Clark University; Hampshire College; Harvard University, Countway Medical, Lamont and Radcliffe College; University of Massachusetts; Tufts University
Michigan	Central Michigan University; Eastern Michigan University; Grand Valley State College; Michigan Technological University; University of Michigan, General and Undergraduate; Northern Michigan University; Wayne University, Medical.
Minnesota	University of Minnesota, General
Mississippi	------
Missouri	Linda Hall Library; University of Missouri at Columbia; University of Missouri at Rolla; University of Missouri at Kansas City; Stephens College; Washington University
Montana	------
Nebraska	University of Nebraska, Agriculture
Nevada	University of Nevada, Reno
New Hampshire	------
New Jersey	Princeton University, Storage; Rider College
New Mexico	College of Santa Fe
New York	Cazenovia College; Columbia University, Law; Cornell University; Hamilton College; Hofstra University; Rochester University; State University of New York at Albany; Wells College
North Carolina	Elon College; Duke University; University of North Carolina, General and Undergraduate
North Dakota	------
Ohio	Baldwin Wallace College; Bowling Green State University; Case Western Reserve University; Findlay College; John Carroll University; Ohio Northern University; Wooster College

Oklahoma	Oklahoma Christian College; Oklahoma State University; University of Oklahoma; Oral Roberts University
Oregon	Lewis and Clark University; Oregon State University; University of Oregon, Science and General; Portland State College; Reed College; Southern Oregon College
Pennsylvania	Beaver College; Bryn Mawr College; Haverford College; Kutztown State College; Lafayette College; Lehigh University, Science; University of Pennsylvania; Pittsburgh University; Temple University, Law and General
Rhode Island	Brown University
South Carolina	Clemson University
South Dakota	University of South Dakota
Tennessee	Austin Peay State College; Belmont College; Fiske University; Scarritt College; Vanderbilt University, General, Science, Law and Medicine
Texas	Abilene Christian College; Hardin Simmons University; University of Houston, Law; McMurray College; North Texas State; Rice University; Southern Methodist University, Science and Law; Southwestern University; University of Texas at El Paso; Undergraduate library at the University of Texas
Utah	Brigham Young University; University of Utah, Business, General and Law
Vermont	Bennington College
Virginia	The Citadel; Washington and Lee University
Washington	Eastern Washington State College; Pacific Lutheran University; Washington State University; University of Washington; Western Washington State College
Washington, D.C.	American University; Georgetown University
Wisconsin	Beloit College; University of Wisconsin at Madison, Agriculture and Medicine; University of Wisconsin at Milwaukee
Wyoming	University of Wyoming
Canada	Guelph University; Simon Fraser University; University of Waterloo; Waterloo Lutheran University
France	Aix-en-Provence University, Letters and Droit; Caen University; University of Lyon; University of Marseille, Science and Social Science; University of Nice, Science and Letters; Orsay University
Germany	Aachen University; Bonn University; University of Frankfurt; Giessen University; Mainz University; Saarbrücken University; Stuttgart University; Würzburgh University
Great Britain	University of Birmingham; East Anglia University; Edinburgh University; Essex University; Exeter University;

Glasgow University; Keele University; Kent University; Lancaster University; Oxford University, Law; Sussex University; Warwick University; York University

Norway   University of Bergen; University of Oslo

Sweden   Chalmers Technological University; University of Gothenberg

Appendix II
Photograph Acknowledgments

California	Occidental College, Joe Friezer, Los Angeles; San Diego State College, Photographic Services, Audio-Visual Department, San Diego State College
Colorado	Southern Colorado State College, Rush J. McCoy, Golden
Connecticut	Yale University, Beinecke Library, Ezra Stoller Associates, Rye, New York
Indiana	Indiana University, Louis Checkman, Jersey City, New Jersey, and Eggers and Higgins, Architects
Iowa	Grinnell College, Baltazar Korab
Missouri	Washington University, Herb Weitman, St. Louis; Washington University, Hedrick Blessing
New York	Cazenovia College, Joseph Marchetti, Philadelphia, Pennsylvania
New Zealand	Auckland University, Vahry Photograph Ltd.
Pennsylvania	Beaver College, Joseph Marchetti; Temple University, Lawrence S. Williams, Inc., Upper Darby, Pennsylvania
Texas	University of Texas at El Paso, Darst-Ireland Photograph, El Paso, Texas

Appendix III
References Cited

American National Standards Institute. *Storage Processed Silver-Gelatin Micro-film, Practice for Storage.* 1970, N.Y., A.N.A.I. (P.H. 5.4–1970)

Ellsworth, Ralph E., *Planning the College and University Library Building,* 2nd edition, Pruett Press, Inc., Boulder, 1969.

Ibid., *The Economics of Book Storage,* Scarecrow Press, Inc. and the Association of Research Libraries, 1969.

Feller, R.L., "The Deteriorating Effects of Light on Museum Objects," *Museum News,* vol. 42, June 1964, *Technical Supplement,* p. VI–VIII.

Fussler, Herman H., *Patterns in the Use of Books in Large Research Libraries,* University of Chicago, 1969.

Holmes, Donald C., *Determination of the Environmental Conditions Required for a Library for the Effective Utilization of Microforms.* Wash., D.C., Assoc. of Research Libraries, Nov. 1970, An Interim Report, Contract No. PEC-0-8-080-786-4612 (095), U.S. Office of Education.

Libraries At Large: Tradition, Innovation and the National Interest. Edited by D.M. Knight, E.S. Nourse, N.Y., Bowker, 1969, Chapter VII.

Mason, Ellsworth, "Beinecke Siamese Twins . . .", *College and Research Libraries,* vol. 26, May 1935, p. 199–212.

Metcalf, Keyes D., *Planning Academic and Research Library Buildings,* McGraw Hill, 1965.

Ibid., *Library Lighting,* Assoc. of Research Libraries, Wash., D.C., 1970.

Morse, P.M., *Library Effectiveness . . . ,* M.I.T. Press, 1968.

Reichmann, F. & Tharpe, J.M., *Determination of an Effective System of Bibliographic Control of Microform Publications,* Wash., D.C., Assoc. of Research Libraries, Nov., 1970, An Interim Report, Contract No. PEC-0-8-080-786-4612 (095), U.S. Office of Education.

Tebbel, J., "Libraries in Miniature: a New Era Begins," *Saturday Review,* January 9, 1971, p. 41–42.

Toffler, Alvin, *Bricks and Mortarboards,* N.Y., Educational Facilities Laboratories, Inc., 1964.

Weber, David C., "Design of a Microtext Reading Room," *UNESCO Bulletin for Libraries,* 20:303–8, N., 1966.

Index to Photographs